EVERNOTE
AS A LAW PRACTICE TOOL

Heidi Alexander

ABALAW
PRACTICE
DIVISION
The Business of Practicing Law

Printed in the United States of America.

20 19 18 17 16 5 4 3 2 1

Library of Congress Cataloging-in-Publication Data
Names: Alexander, Heidi S., author.
Title: Evernote as a law practice tool / Heidi Alexander.
Description: Chicago : American Bar Association, [2016] | Includes bibliographical references.
Identifiers: LCCN 2016052316 (print) | LCCN 2016054752 (ebook) | ISBN 9781634254168 (print) | ISBN 9781634254175 (ePub)
Subjects: LCSH: Practice of law—United States—Automation. | Evernote. | Note-taking—Computer programs. | Time management—Computer programs. | File organization (Computer science)—Computer programs. | Personal information management—Computer programs. | Mobile computing—Law and legislation—United States.
Classification: LCC KF320.A9 A425 2016 (print) | LCC KF320.A9 (ebook) | DDC 340.0285/557—dc23
LC record available at https://lccn.loc.gov/2016052316

Contents

Preface

Years ago, I adopted Evernote into my own practice and, as a result, witnessed an exponential increase in my productivity, both personally and professionally. To this day, I use it as my primary productivity and organizational tool. I cannot even begin to imagine what my life would look like without it!

Odds are that if you are reading this book, you also have an interest in running your practice (and your life) in a more efficient manner. By implementing Evernote into your workflow, you will do just that. This book will make the case for Evernote as an effective law practice tool, demonstrate how to use it on a daily basis, and give you countless tips and tricks to get the most out of the service.

As a former litigator turned practice management advisor to solo and small law firms, I know just how busy you are. And, as tempted as you may be to spend the next few hours poring over the contents of this book (am I right?), that may not be the best use of your time. I've read a great number of software guidebooks, and I have rarely completed an entire book in one sitting. The way I prefer to approach a book of this sort is to begin by reading just enough to provide an adequate foundation to my use of the product. Then I dig into the product, using the book as a reference guide while experimenting and becoming proficient in my use.

That's how I've organized this book for you, beginning with an attempt to convince you to use Evernote, then laying out the core features, and from there progressing into the heart of the product and how it can be used to increase efficiencies in your practice. If you are new to Evernote, I encourage you to continue reading through the first chapter, which describes what Evernote is and why it's useful for lawyers. Immediately thereafter, sign up for an account at www.evernote.com. Yes, put the book down and see what I'm talking about for yourself. Then, come back to the book and read it in chunks. Each chapter provides another useful tidbit that you'll be able to apply to your own Evernote use. If you are already an Evernote power user, you can skip directly to the chapter that suits you, in the order of your preference. Eventually, you'll want to hit every chapter, because I've included bonus power user tips just for you.

I've written this guide from my perspective as both an avid Evernote user and practice management advisor. As such, I've suggested real-life strategies based on those I use every day, as well as techniques that are particularly useful for lawyers. In addition to practical strategies, the book aims to make implementation of Evernote in your practice a painless process. It's one thing to contemplate incorporating a new product or technique into your practice, but it's a whole other thing to actually do it.

Now, without further ado, I give you your trusted guide to using Evernote in your law practice.

Acknowledgments

Thanks to Laura Calloway for serving as my liaison to the American Bar Association Law Practice Division Publishing Board and providing her experienced assistance whenever needed. Thanks to my reviewers, Laura Calloway and Tom Mighell, for their diligent edits and suggestions to help ensure this book's relevance and usefulness to the legal profession.

A special thanks to all the lawyers who contributed by sharing their own uses and tips for Evernote with readers. Those lawyers include Joseph Bahgat, Ben Carter, Jay Fleischman, Katie Floyd, Philippe Doyle Gray, John Harding, Jeffrey Lewis, Cat Moon, and Jacob Small.

About the Author

Heidi S. Alexander, Esq. has dedicated her career to helping entre-
preneurs build successful businesses. Early in her career, she worked
with a women's business assistance center, spearheading economic
development by assisting women to launch and grow businesses.
She went on to become a lawyer; serving, in law school, as the editor-
in-chief of the law review; clerking for a justice on the highest court of
New Jersey; and practicing law at a small firm in Boston.

Aligning her interests in entrepreneurship, technology, and the
law, Heidi opened a consulting business focused on technology and
marketing for law firms. Ultimately, that led to her current work as
a Law Practice Management Advisor and Director of Practice Management Services for Lawyers Concerned for Lawyers in Massachusetts. In this role, she advises lawyers on practice management
matters, provides guidance in implementing new law office technol-
ogies, and helps lawyers develop healthy and sustainable practices.
She frequently makes presentations to the legal community, contrib-
utes to publications on law practice management and technology,
and collaborates with bar associations, including having served on
the American Bar Association's TECHSHOW Planning Board.

You can follow Heidi on Twitter (@HeidiAlexander) and LinkedIn
(www.linkedin.com/in/HeidiSarahAlexander).

An Introduction to Evernote

I presume that if you've picked up a copy of this book, you have at least a vague idea of what Evernote is and what it can do. Just in case, this chapter provides the framework for the remainder of the book by describing the product, why it is so powerful, and how you can get it.

1.1 What Is Evernote?

Before we can jump into how to use Evernote in practice, you first need to understand just what it is. Here's how some have described it:

> It's your brain offloaded to a server. It's Google for the Web of your life. It's a spotlight on the dark matter of your universe. It's a tool for converting your smartphone from a time killer to a time saver.[1] (Phil Libin, co-founder and former CEO of Evernote)

---

1. Inc.com, *Evernote: 2011 Company of the Year*, http://www.inc.com/magazine /201112/evernote-2011-company-of-the-year.html.

A suite of software and services, designed for note taking and archiving.[2] (Wikipedia)

As one workspace that lives across your phone, tablet, and computer, Evernote is the place you write free from distraction, collect information, find what you need, and present your ideas to the world.[3] (Evernote website)

Evernote is a free app for your smartphone and computer that stores everything you could possible imagine losing track of.[4] (*Business Insider*)

And indeed, it's precisely the co-founder Phil Libin's vision—a memory aid for just about everything we do. Say goodbye to hours spent searching for those meeting notes you saved somewhere on your computer or mobile device, or that to-do list you think you put in your briefcase, and say hello to Evernote, the single program that lets you access important data with the click of a button and save important information wherever and whenever you need.

Evernote is available to anyone with Internet access, and there's no need for extensive training to use the program. Thanks to the company's thoughtful and painstaking development, Evernote gives you a robust yet simple and intuitive set of functions, including note taking; saving, storing, and organizing data; sharing and collaborating with others; annotating; and more.

1.2 Where Did It Come From?

Evernote got its start like many other tech companies—from a bunch of folks in Silicon Valley conjuring up ideas, working the technology, and making the right connections. Evernote stemmed from an idea to create a technology that would serve as a memory aid, but in an organized and productive manner. After years of coordination and development, in 2008 Evernote launched a private beta product that soon after, due to demand, went public.[5]

---

2. Wikipedia: Evernote, http://en.wikipedia.org/wiki/Evernote.
3. Evernote.com, *About Evernote*, https://evernote.com/corp.
4. BusinessInsider.com, *You're Nuts If You're Not Using This App to Organize All Your Stuff*, http://www.businessinsider.com/evernote-2012-1.
5. Inc.com, *Evernote: 2011 Company of the Year.*

Since then, Evernote has received loads of venture capital funding, now employs hundreds of employees in offices around the world,[6] and has over 100 million users worldwide.[7] Originally offering a free and premium model, Evernote now has a tiered pricing plan[8] (see Evernote Service Levels, the appendix of this book).

1.3 What Can It Do?

Evernote provides an orderly and accessible system to offload and organize information that you don't have immediate use for but can take up valuable space in your brain. The more data you can clear out of your brain, the more brain power you'll have to devote to important processes and tasks presented to you.

Evernote can be used for basic functions such as note taking or saving articles, as well as more sophisticated functions such as annotation or collaboration. One of Evernote's unparalleled features is its Web Clipper, which allows you to save articles and web pages, take screenshots, and bookmark sites directly from your web browser to store and organize in Evernote. No more cutting and pasting web content into a Word document that you'll never remember where it's saved anyhow. Evernote's organizational features, like its notebooks, tags, and search, make your content easily accessible wherever you might be (at your computer or on the run with your mobile device). Further, features such as reminders and checklists aid in daily work projects, keeping you apprised of and on top of your deadlines.

---

6. As part of a restructuring effort, since 2015, Evernote has laid off a number of employees and brought on new senior-level executives. BizJournals.com, *Evernote Cuts 20 Staffers Globally in First Layoffs; Austin Shop Suffers*; TechCrunch.com, *Evernote's Founding CTO Dave Engberg Is Leaving in May*, http://techcrunch.com/2016/03/18 /evernote-brings-in-new-product-marketing-design-and-china-heads-in-exec-overhaul/; TheVerge.com, *Evernote Laying Off 13 Percent of Staff Two Months after CEO Change*, http://www.theverge.com/2015/9/29/9420031/evernote-layoffs-office-closures.
7. Evernote Blog, *We Have 100 Million People to Thank*, https://blog.evernote.com /blog/2014/05/13/evernote-reaches-100-million-users.
8. TechCrunch.com, *Evernote's New Pricing Includes a Cheaper, Middle Tier and a Pricier Top Plan*, http://techcrunch.com/2015/04/29/evernotes-new-pricing-includes -a-cheaper-middle-tier-and-a-pricier-top-plan.

1.4 How Can Lawyers Use It?

Well, you've come to the right place. That's what this book is all about! Using Evernote to organize your legal work could take many forms, but primarily Evernote acts as a central repository for storing information that you need to use in practice. I've written an entire chapter (see Chapter 5) detailing specific uses for saving, organizing, managing, and collaborating in your day-to-day law practice.

Potential uses for lawyers include firm administration and management, marketing plans, case management, legal research, and time management. In addition to my suggestions, I've provided testimonials from a number of lawyers who are Evernote power users to give you even more ideas of how to tailor Evernote to your own practice (see Chapter 7).

1.5 How Do You Get It?

Now that you know what it is and why it can be useful to you, it's time to get started.

Go to www.evernote.com to sign up for a free account. In the appendix of this book, Evernote Service Levels, I address differences between Basic (free), Plus, Premium, and Evernote Business accounts. It's best to start off with a free account before investing in Plus or Premium. Evernote makes upgrading a simple process.

You can access your Evernote account through your web browser, and you can download Evernote to the following desktop and mobile platforms:

- Android
- Apple
- Blackberry
- Windows

Evernote's user interface for each platform is built to complement its respective operating system, thus reducing the learning curve for quicker competency with the program. While each platform is nuanced in its look and feel, Evernote's core features are available on every platform. Accordingly, the concepts of this book will apply to all platforms, but the instructions and screenshots come from the desktop applications for Windows PC and Mac. Chapter 4 specifically addresses the nuances of mobile platforms.

I've chosen to highlight the desktop applications because of their versatility and robust set of features. A beginner can easily learn to navigate Evernote via a standard desktop application menu, while power users can take advantage of the application shortcuts. Further, the desktop versions (regardless of whether you have a free or paid subscription) allow you to view all your notes without an Internet connection because Evernote stores a local copy of your notes on your computer's hard drive. The web platform, in particular, departs from its mobile and desktop companions with a simplified design for distraction-free note taking.

If you are new to Evernote, it's best to get started with the desktop application to learn the ins and outs of the program, and then move on to experimentation with other platforms. What's most important is that you obtain a basic understanding of the product's functions and then apply it to whatever platform you use.

1.6 Where Can I Learn More about It?

Beyond this book, the best places to learn about Evernote and how to use it are Evernote's own Blog and Help & Learning site. The Evernote Blog, available at blog.evernote.com, provides the latest product news, user tips, and specific advice on how to integrate Evernote into your workflow. The Evernote Help & Learning site, available at https://help.evernote.com/hc/en-us/, provides guides, videos, troubleshooting articles, and more. When I need answers to a question, this is where I start. Use the search function to find information on your topic of interest or look for articles related to a particular platform.

1.7 A Note on Instructions, Images, and Shortcuts in This Book

As mentioned previously, this book focuses on the desktop platforms and includes a specific chapter dedicated to mobile use. Evernote provides a downloadable desktop client for Windows PC and Mac. For the most part, each client employs the same set of features, but with slight design deviations (i.e., the location of a certain button or menu item).

All instructions, including discussion of features, use, and organization, will reference the desktop platforms. When necessary, both Windows and Mac instructions are provided.

Images

For simplicity, most screenshots will display the Mac desktop client, except when design variations deviate significantly; in that case, a screenshot from the Windows client will also appear.

Shortcuts

To be most efficient in your use of Evernote, use keyboard shortcuts when possible. Interspersed throughout this book are shortcuts for both Mac and Windows users. Windows shortcuts are self-explanatory. Mac shortcuts are typically abbreviated with symbols. If you are not accustomed to using Mac shortcuts, here is your guide:

^ = Control
⌥ = Option
⇧ = Shift
⌘ = Command

2

Core Features

This chapter provides an overview of Evernote's core features. It's not meant to be a comprehensive listing of all features, which you can find via the Evernote Blog and Help & Learning site. The following features will help you get the most out of Evernote in your law practice.

2.1 Evernote Vocabulary

Workspace

Your workspace is the dashboard that displays your content and gives you access to Evernote tools. See Figure 2.1 (Mac) and Figure 2.2 (Windows). A number of navigation menus appear in your workspace: (1) a standard application menu (i.e., File, Edit, View, etc.) via your computer's menu bar (Mac) or at the very top of the Evernote application window (Windows); (2) a customizable secondary menu (Evernote menu) within the Evernote application itself; (3) a note attribute menu (Note menu); and (4) a note formatting menu (Format menu). Customization of your workspace is discussed in Section 3.8.

FIGURE 2.1
Workspace for Mac Desktop

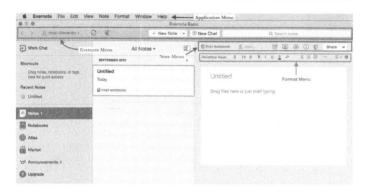

FIGURE 2.2
Workspace for Windows Desktop

Notes

Notes are the heart of Evernote. Notes may contain text, audio, images, documents, e-mails, or web content. Each note displays a title and area for the content (see Figure 2.3). Using tools similar to (but more basic than) those of a word processor, you can format and style the text of a note.

FIGURE 2.3
Single Note

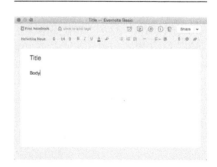

Notebooks

Notebooks are organizational tools for your notes. Notebooks are similar to electronic folders that contain individual files. Notebooks contain notes. Like your electronic filing system, multiple notebooks may be gathered together, within one single notebook, called a notebook stack. Understand, however, that whereas your electronic filing system may contain many levels of folders within folders, Evernote only allows for a single level—notebooks within a single notebook stack. Figure 2.4 displays a list of notebooks and notebook stacks.

FIGURE 2.4

Notebooks

Tags

Tags provide a further level of organization. A tag might categorize certain notes within one notebook or among multiple notebooks. For example, as demonstrated in Figure 2.5, if you saved case law research within a notebook labeled Employment Discrimination, you might tag those cases with the labels Disability, Sex, Age, and so on for further differentiation. Figure 2.6 shows a list of tags.

FIGURE 2.5
Note Tags

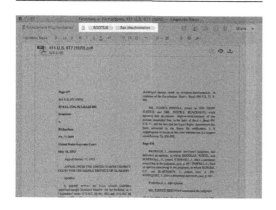

FIGURE 2.6
Tag List

Some Evernote users swear by notebooks only, while others use only tags. Some use both notebooks and tags. There are advantages to each method. In Chapter 5, you'll find suggestions for different uses of both notebooks and tags in your legal work.

POWER USER TIP

One advantage of using tags is that you have up to 100,000 per account, whereas you are limited to 250 notebooks. An individual note may contain a maximum of 100 tags, but it can be assigned to only a single notebook (however, you may copy a note to multiple notebooks). Further, tags may be nested in multiple levels (see Figure 2.7), whereas a group of notebooks can only be organized into a single notebook stack. At the date of this writing, however, nested tags do not appear as nested on an iOS device.

FIGURE 2.7

Nested Tags

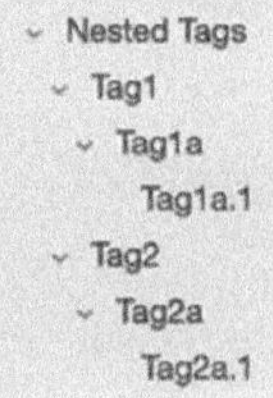

> Nested Tags
> Tag1
> Tag1a
> Tag1a.1
> Tag2
> Tag2a
> Tag2a.1

2.2 Sync

A core feature of Evernote is its ability to sync across platforms. All your content is stored in the cloud (don't worry, we'll talk security in Chapter 6), with the exception of local notebooks (explained in Section 3.1). Therefore, when you input information into one device it will appear, in real time, on all other devices, even if you use a variety of operating systems (i.e., Windows, Mac, iOS, Android). This feature eliminates multiple data entry and enables you to take your entire Evernote workspace on the go. You can configure sync to occur at different time frames (i.e., every 5, 15, 30 minutes, or on the hour) or you can sync manually.

Mac

To configure sync via Mac, select Evernote from the application menu > Preferences > Sync (see Figures 2.8 and 2.9).

FIGURE 2.8
Preferences (Mac)

FIGURE 2.9
Sync Options (Mac)

Windows

To configure sync via Windows, select Tools from the application menu > Options > Sync (see Figures 2.10 and 2.11).

FIGURE 2.10
Tools (Windows)

FIGURE 2.11
Sync Options (Windows)

Regardless of how your sync is configured, you can always sync manually via the icon in your Evernote menu (see Figure 2.12).

FIGURE 2.12
Manual Sync Button

> ## POWER USER TIP
>
> While Evernote syncs across platforms, unless you have a wireless connection for your mobile device, you cannot, by default, view your notes. With Evernote Plus and Premium, you can choose to download all notes or certain notebooks to view offline. The notes or selected notebooks are then synced and downloaded directly to your device. For more on Plus and Premium perks, see the appendix.

2.3 Reminders

For time-sensitive notes, such as an upcoming task or court filing, you can set reminders to notify you on a certain date. To set a reminder, click on the clock icon in the Note menu and then on Add a Date (see Figure 2.13). Use Evernote's quick options to set the reminder for Tomorrow, In a Week, or a particular date (see Figure 2.14).

FIGURE 2.13	**FIGURE 2.14**
Set a Reminder	Choose a Date

Once you've added your reminder, it will appear in the Reminders list above your note titles (see Figure 2.15). This list appears when you view All Notes and within each Notebook. You can sort

FIGURE 2.15
Reminders List

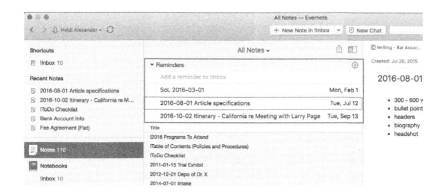

reminders by date, upcoming, and recently completed. When you mark a reminder as complete, Evernote checks off the reminder but does not delete the note. You can add another reminder after you've cleared the first reminder. At the time of this writing, you cannot add multiple reminders or set recurring reminders in Evernote.

To receive notifications for your reminders, you can set Evernote Preferences (Mac)/Options (Windows) to send e-mails when notes are due. See Figure 2.16 (Mac) and Figure 2.17 (Windows). You can also turn on Evernote notifications on your computer and mobile devices.

FIGURE 2.16
Turn on E-mail Notifications (Mac)

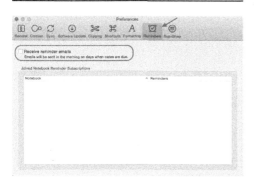

FIGURE 2.17
Turn on E-mail Notifications (Windows)

2.4 Internal Note Links

Internal note links provide a way to create one-click references to other notes within Evernote. For example, a note containing a deposition outline might use internal note links to reference exhibits and research saved in Evernote (more on specific litigation and case management uses in Section 5.2). You can also use internal note links to create a table of contents—for example, to quickly refer to the firm policies contained in your Policies and Procedures Notebook.

Create a Note Link

Create a note link by right-clicking on the note (or multiple notes) you'd like to link to and then selecting Copy Note Link (see Figure 2.18). Or, go to the application menu under Note and select Copy Note Link (see Figure 2.19). Then, paste the note link (or multiple note links) into another note.

FIGURE 2.18
Right-Click, Copy Note Link

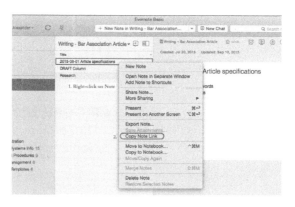

FIGURE 2.19
Note Menu, Copy Note Link

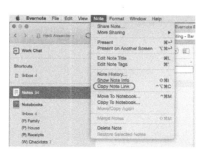

POWER USER TIP

Bypass a few clicks by creating a note link using a keyboard short-cut. For Mac users, the keyboard shortcut is ^⌥⌘C. For Windows users, the shortcut is ALT + N (pulls up the Note menu) and then L (L selects Copy Note Link).

Create a Table of Contents

Using the note-linking functionality described earlier, Evernote also has a Create a Table of Contents button that will create a new note with links to all the notes you have selected. First, select multiple notes (⌘ + click with Mac; Ctrl + click with Windows) and then select Create Table of Contents Note (see Figure 2.20). This creates a new note with links to all of the preselected notes (see Figure 2.21).

FIGURE 2.20
Create a Table of Contents

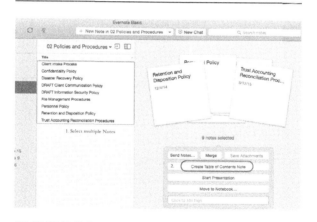

FIGURE 2.21
Table of Contents Note

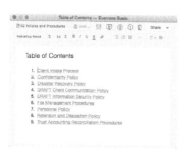

2.5 Merge Notes

Rather than wholesale copying of content from one note to another, use Evernote's merge function to do it seamlessly. Merge notes by selecting the notes you'd like to merge (⌘ + click with Mac; Ctrl + click with Windows) and then selecting Merge (see Figure 2.22). The result is one note containing all selected notes (see Figure 2.23). The new note title will adopt the most recently modified note (for Mac users) or the first selected note (for Windows users). All additional titles will appear as headers within the note.

FIGURE 2.22
Merge Notes

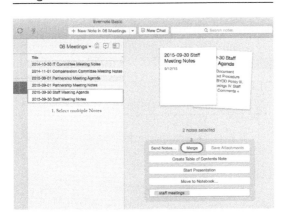

FIGURE 2.23
Note after Merge

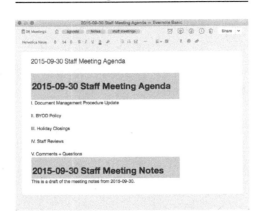

2.6 Annotation

You can annotate images and PDF files with Evernote's annotation tool. You can also create a PDF of an existing note and annotate it. Whereas image annotation is available to all account holders, PDF annotation is available for Premium users only. Basic account holders can use the PDF annotation feature ten times before requiring an upgrade to Premium.

To annotate a note, look for the "a" button. Mac users can choose to annotate an individual image or PDF, or to annotate the entire note as a PDF (see Figure 2.24). Windows users can hover over any image or attached PDF and click the Annotate button (for images) or "a" that appears in the pop-up toolbar (for PDFs; see Figure 2.25).

FIGURE 2.24
Annotate (Mac)

FIGURE 2.25
Annotate (Windows)

Evernote provides a variety of basic annotation tools, including arrows, lines and shapes, text, highlighting, and stamps, as well as pixelate (blur), crop, and resize tools (see Figure 2.26). The type of tools available may differ slightly depending on whether you are annotating an image or PDF. Note that Evernote's annotation tools are limited as compared to a robust PDF program, such as Adobe Acrobat.

FIGURE 2.26
Annotation Tools

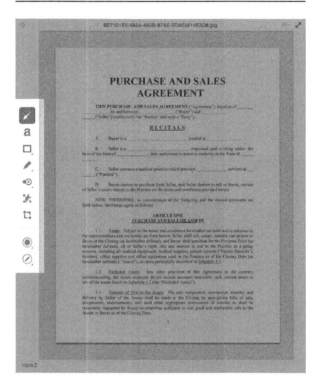

Evernote also provides an annotation summary feature to display how many times a certain type of annotation has been used as well as clips of all annotations in the file. When turned on—see Figure 2.27 (Mac) and Figure 2.28 (Windows)—the summary appears appended to the PDF as the first page (see Figure 2.29).

FIGURE 2.27
Turn On/Off Annotation Summary (Mac)

FIGURE 2.28
Turn On/Off Annotation Summary (Windows)

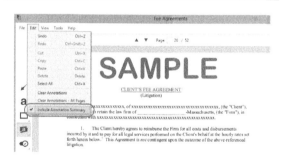

FIGURE 2.29
Annotation Summary

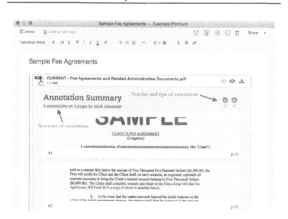

2.7 Trash

When you delete notes, similar to your operating system, Evernote's Trash notebook keeps them until you manually delete them. Evernote's Trash notebook appears at the very end of the notebook list in your sidebar. (You can also find your Trash notebook by clicking on the Notebooks icon in the sidebar.) To empty the entire Trash notebook, select the notebook, right-click, and select Empty Trash (see Figure 2.30).

To permanently delete individual notes from the trash, open the Trash notebook and select the individual note or notes that you wish to erase. Select Erase Note(s) (see Figure 2.31). If you accidentally trashed a note (but did not use Erase to remove the note permanently) and wish to restore it, you can do this via the Trash notebook. Open the Trash notebook, select the individual note or notes, and then select Restore Note(s) (see Figure 2.31).

FIGURE 2.30
Empty Trash

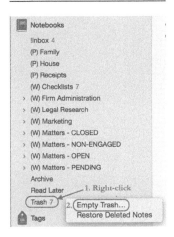

FIGURE 2.31
Erase or Restore a Note

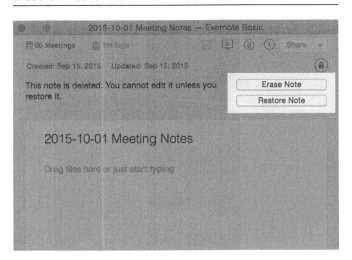

POWER USER TIP

For notes that you'd like to remove from a certain Notebook, but may hold some future relevance and thus you don't feel comfortable deleting them forever, you may want to create an Archive notebook. Evernote allows you to store a large amount of notes, so you need not worry about space limitations (and if, down the road, you do, then you can prune notes from your Archive notebook). Because Evernote's search feature (discussed in Section 3.7) does not index your Trash notebook, placing notes into an Archive notebook rather than in the Trash will allow you to rediscover those notes via a search.

2.8 Presentation Mode

Presentation mode allows you to display content from your notes in full screen on your computer, mobile device, or secondary screen. When using presentation mode with a second screen, you can make edits to your note on your primary device that will be reflected in real time on your second screen. You might use presentation mode to review notes stored in Evernote, such as a firm policy with staff or a client document during a meeting. To start presentation mode, select a note to present and then click on the Presentation button on the Note menu (see Figure 2.32). Use the pointer tool to emphasize certain portions during your presentation. Additional settings give you control over the layout of your presentation, allowing you to break up long notes into discrete viewing sections (see Figure 2.33). Presentation mode is available only for Premium users and can be used with Evernote desktop or mobile platforms, but not via web browser.

FIGURE 2.32
Presentation Button
(Single Note)

FIGURE 2.33
Presentation Tools

2014-12-31 P & S Agreement

POWER USER TIP

To jump from note to note during a presentation, as you would with a slide presentation, first create a table of contents with the notes you plan to display and then start your presentation. Click on a specific note link from the table of contents to display that note. Mac users can use the Shortcut command ⌘[(open bracket) to quickly return to the table of contents.

3

Creating and Managing Content

Now let's take those features described in Chapter 2 and put them to use. This chapter demonstrates how to organize your workspace; create, view, and manage content; and add content from external sources.

3.1 Creating Notebooks and Stacks

Creating a Notebook

As with many of Evernote's features, there is more than one way to create a notebook.

Option 1: From any view, select File from the application menu and click on New Notebook. When adding a new notebook from the Evernote desktop platform, you'll have the option of creating a synchronized or local notebook. A local notebook will remain only on your computer and will not sync across devices. For easy access to your content on multiple devices, I recommend selecting Synchronized Notebook. This process is demonstrated in Figure 3.1.

Option 2: Click on the Notebooks icon in your sidebar to view all Notebooks, then select + New Notebook in the upper left-hand corner (see Figure 3.2). You can also get to Notebooks view by going to

FIGURE 3.1
Create a New Notebook from the Application Menu

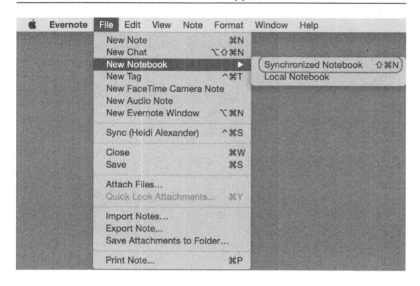

FIGURE 3.2
Create a New Notebook from Notebook List

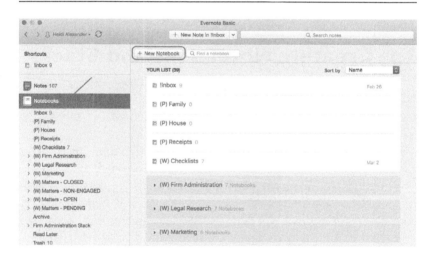

the application menu, clicking on View and then Notebooks; or, by using a shortcut: ⌥⌘2 (Mac) or Ctrl + Shift + Alt + B (Windows).

Option 3: Use a shortcut to create a notebook. For Mac users, the shortcut is ⇧⌘N. For Windows users, the shortcut is Ctrl + Shift + N.

Once you've created a new notebook, name the notebook (for more on naming and organization, see Section 3.5).

Creating Notebook Stacks

Sometimes you will want to group multiple notebooks together, such as all notebooks related to the administration of your firm. This is called a stack. The easiest way organize your notebooks into stacks is within the Notebooks view. To create a new stack, drag and drop one notebook on top of another. That will create a new notebook stack with your two notebooks inside. Then, right-click on the notebook stack to rename it. To add notebooks to an existing stack, drag and drop notebooks onto the stack.

Mac desktop users can also create a new stack by right-clicking on a notebook (in Notebooks view) and selecting Add to Stack and then New Stack. A notebook stack will be created with only that one notebook inside. You can add notebooks by dragging and dropping or by right-clicking on a notebook and selecting Add to Stack.

3.2 Adding a Note and Note Tags

Adding a Note

Similar to when creating a notebook, there are a few ways that you can add a new note.

Option 1: Click on New Note from the Evernote menu. See Figure 3.3 (Mac) and Figure 3.4 (Windows).

FIGURE 3.3
Add New Note from Evernote Menu (Mac)

FIGURE 3.4
Add New Note from Evernote Menu (Windows)

Option 2: Select File from the application menu, and click on New Note (see Figure 3.5).

FIGURE 3.5
Add New Note from Application Menu

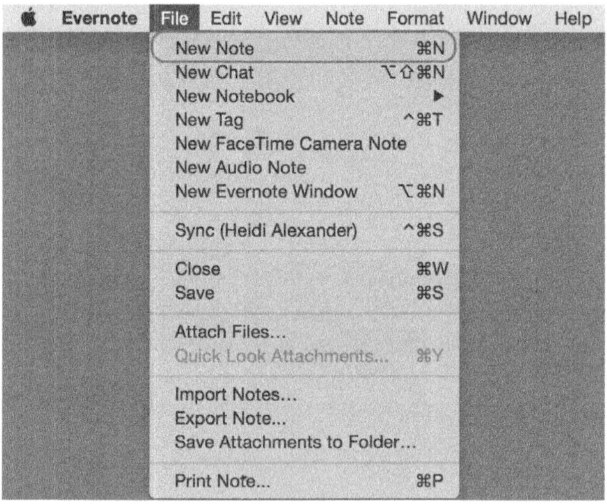

Option 3: Use a shortcut. For Mac users, the shortcut is ⌘N. For Windows users, the shortcut is Ctrl + N.

POWER USER TIP

Evernote for Mac provides a computer menu bar item with Quick Note functionality (see Figure 3.6). From the top of your Mac, select the Evernote icon and add a new note with text/images/attachments, take a screen shot, or record audio. The shortcut for this feature is ^⌘N. Any notes saved via Quick Note go directly to your default notebook.

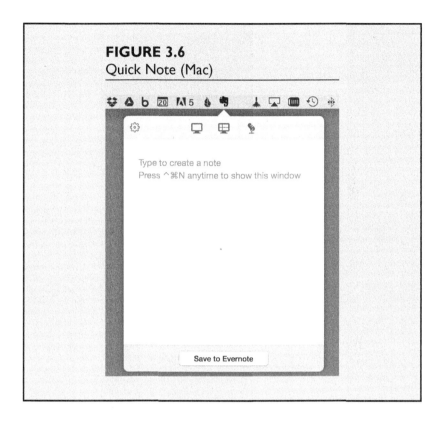

FIGURE 3.6
Quick Note (Mac)

Assigning a Note to a Notebook

By default, your new note will appear in your default notebook. You can add a note to a particular notebook by either creating a new note from within that notebook or by selecting the notebook from the note menu (see Figures 3.7 through 3.10).

FIGURE 3.7
Find Notebook in Note Menu (Mac)

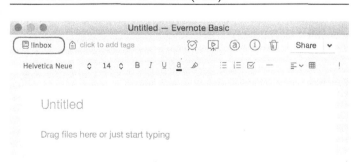

FIGURE 3.8
Notebook from Note Menu (Mac)

FIGURE 3.9
Find Notebook in Note Menu (Windows)

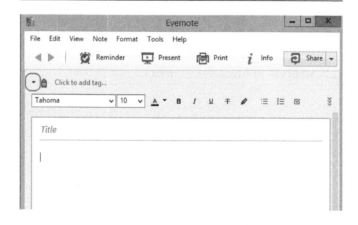

FIGURE 3.10
Select Notebook from Note Menu (Windows)

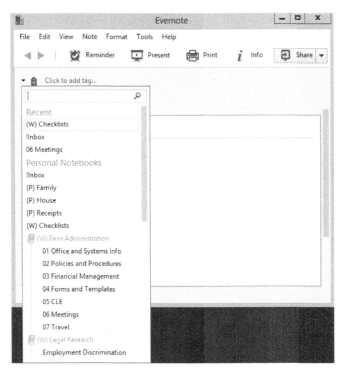

Your default notebook will be labeled with your username until you rename it. It's a good idea to rename your default notebook to Inbox because that's where most of the data you collect will end up before you move it into specific notebooks. Also, use a special one-character prefix (such as !, @, *, or .). Placing a special character in front of any Evernote element (note, notebook, or tag) will ensure that when sorted by name, it appears above other entries that begin with numbers or letters. Renaming your default notebook to !Inbox ensures that it will always appear at the top of your Notebook List.

Note Attributes

The Note menu at the top of each note contains a number of attributes (see Figure 3.11). To view those attributes, ensure that your window is expanded wide enough to show all attributes. Attributes include the following:

1. Notebook—Shows the notebook where the note resides.
2. Tags—Click here to add tags.
3. Reminder—Set, complete, or remove a reminder.
4. Presentation (Premium)—Start a presentation.
5. Annotation (Premium)—Mark up the note.
6. Information—Provides the title, notebook, when the note was created, when it was updated, a URL for sharing (if shared), the location where it was created, when it was last synced, its attachment status, size (MB/KB, word and character count), the author, and note history.
7. Trash—Places the note in the Trash.
8. Share—Shares a note or notebook and manages note permissions.
9. Formatting Bar—Contains formatting and styling features such as fonts, styles, bullets, checkboxes, charts, and more.

FIGURE 3.11
Note Attributes

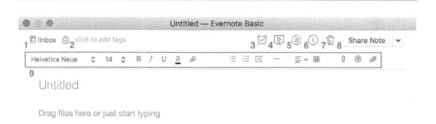

Note Tags

Tags allow you to further organize your notes. By assigning multiple tags to a note, you provide additional note descriptors for search purposes and to make connections to other notes with the same tags. Due to the limitations on the number of notebooks, some users choose to use tags in addition to or in place of notebooks. In Chapter 5, I discuss using tags for organizing your legal work.

To add a tag to a note, click on the Tag attribute in the Note menu (see Figure 3.12). You can add a new tag or select an existing tag.

You can search by tags to reveal all notes with a certain tag. You can also view tags as you would notebooks—both in your sidebar and in the full screen (see Figure 3.13). To view full screen, go to

FIGURE 3.12
Add a Tag

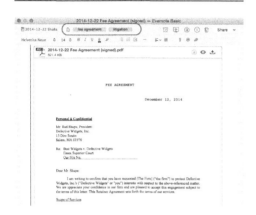

FIGURE 3.13
Sidebar and Full-Screen View

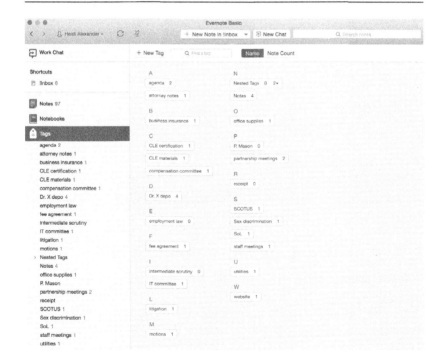

your sidebar and click on Tags, go to the application menu and click on View and then Tags View, or use a shortcut: ⌥⌘3 (Mac) or Ctrl + Shift + Alt + T (Windows).

POWER USER TIP

You can create a multilevel hierarchy of tags by nesting tags (see Figure 3.14). In the full-screen tag view, you can nest tags just like you'd create a notebook stack. Drag and drop a tag onto another tag to nest it.

FIGURE 3.14
Nested Tags from Sidebar and Full-Screen View

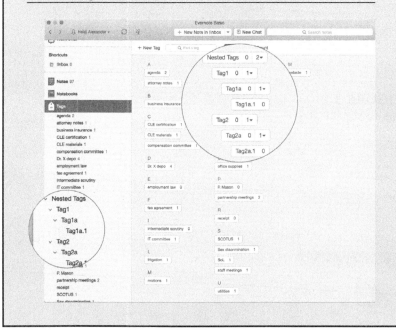

3.3 Adding Content to a Note

Notes support a variety of content, including text, audio, images, documents, web pages, and e-mails.

Adding content can be accomplished in a number of ways. The following sections demonstrate how to:

- Add text
- Add audio

- Add documents and images
- Save content from the web
- Save content via e-mail

Adding Text and Formatting

To add text to a note, simply create a new note or open an existing note and begin typing. Text may be formatted via the Format menu or by selecting Format from the main application menu. You must first place your cursor in the note title or text box before the Note formatting menu will appear. Basic word processing formatting and styling options are available, including tools for creating tables, lists, and links. You can set the default fonts from your word processing program Preferences (Mac)/Options (Windows).

A checkbox styling tool is also offered to both desktop and mobile users. With this tool, you can create a to-do list and check off the items as they are completed (see Figure 3.15). You can also search for incomplete to-dos with Evernote's search feature (for more on Search, see Section 3.7).

FIGURE 3.15
Create To-Do List

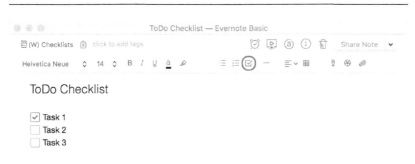

Windows users have the unique ability to create a handwritten note by selecting Ink Note from the Evernote menu or using the shortcut Ctrl + Shift + L (see Figure 3.16). A special Ink Note formatting menu will appear with different writing tools and colors (see Figure 3.17).

FIGURE 3.16
New Ink Note from Evernote Menu (Windows)

FIGURE 3.17
Ink Note Formatting Menu (Windows)

Adding Audio

To record and add an audio clip to your note, select the microphone button from the formatting menu (see Figure 3.18). You can record multiple audio clips into the note. After adding audio clips, you can play and download them as WAV files.

FIGURE 3.18
Add Audio

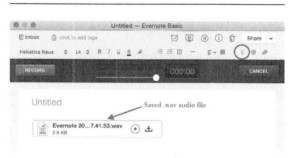

Adding Documents and Images

To attach a document or image to a note, click on the paperclip button in the formatting menu (see Figure 3.19). A new window will prompt you to select the document or image from your hard drive. You can attach multiple documents or images.

You can also add a file by dragging and dropping the document or image into a note.

FIGURE 3.19
Add Attachment

Files within a note will appear inline or as an attachment link. You can change how the files appear in Preferences (Mac)/Options (Windows) or by right-clicking on the file and selecting View Inline or View as Attachment. Files within notes may be viewed and downloaded.

Take a Snapshot

You can use your computer's webcam to take a picture and save it to your note. Mac users can do so by clicking the shutter button in the Format menu (see Figure 3.20). Windows users should select New Webcam Note from the Evernote menu (see Figure 3.21).

FIGURE 3.20
Take a Snapshot (Mac)

FIGURE 3.21
Take a Snapshot (Windows)

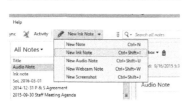

Save Documents Directly from Your Computer

Another way to add documents and images to your notes is by doing so directly from your computer, rather than from within Evernote. You might use this option when you don't have Evernote open and wish to save content from your computer quickly to a note. Mac users can use this one-step option to turn a file into a PDF and save it into Evernote. Windows users might find this option helpful to import batches of files into Evernote. Both Mac and Windows platforms will require some setup to make this work.

Mac

On the Mac, you can save files to Evernote by using Mac's print function. Open any application that allows for printing, and then select File > Print (or use the shortcut ⌘P). Under the PDF drop-down menu in the bottom left-hand corner, select Save to Evernote (see Figure 3.22).

FIGURE 3.22
Save to Evernote from Print Dialog (Mac)

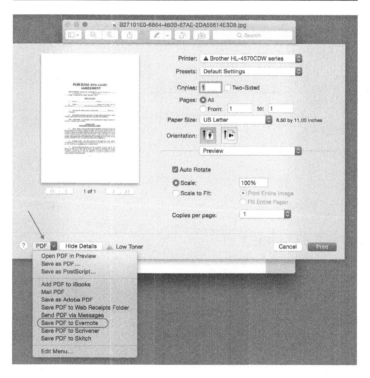

The document or image will be saved as a PDF into your default notebook. If Save to Evernote is not currently an option under PDF, simply add it by selecting Edit Menu in the PDF drop-down menu, click the plus sign (+), and then find Evernote in your applications and click Open. Save to Evernote will then appear in your print dialog box options.

POWER USER TIP

On a Mac, you can add Evernote to your Share menu so that you can right-click on any file, select Share and then Evernote to save a file to Evernote. Figure 3.23 demonstrates how to add the Evernote share extension to your Mac (you'll find your Share menu in Preferences > Extensions) and Figure 3.24 shows how to use the Share menu to save a file to Evernote.

FIGURE 3.23
Add Evernote Share Extension (Mac)

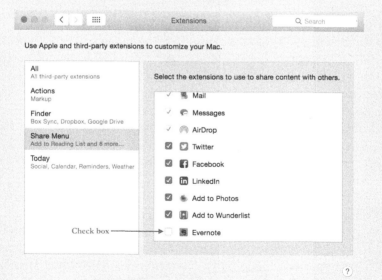

FIGURE 3.24
Share to Evernote Using Share Menu (Mac)

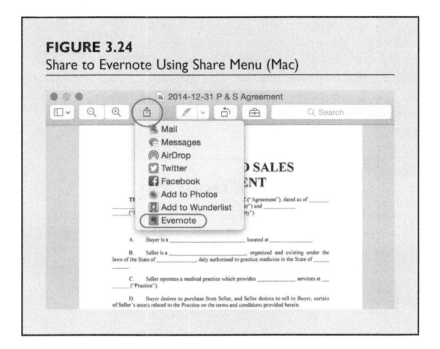

Windows

In Windows, you'll use its import folders feature to automatically add files to Evernote. First, you'll need to create a new folder and name it Add to Evernote (see Figure 3.25). Then, from your Evernote application menu, select Tools > Import Folders and click Add to create a new import folder (see Figure 3.26). Now, still in Evernote, find the Add to Evernote folder in the Browse For Folder dialog box and click OK (see Figure 3.27). Any file you place into this folder on your computer will then be saved to your default notebook in Evernote.

In the Evernote Windows desktop platform, you can set up multiple import folders to save into different notebooks. Use Tools > Import Folders settings to change the import location of a certain folder on your desktop. You can also change the settings to delete files from your desktop import folders after they have been imported into Evernote. In import folders settings, click on Keep in the Source column, then on Delete, and then on OK (see Figure 3.28).

FIGURE 3.25
Create New
Folder (Windows)

FIGURE 3.26
Tools > Import Folders (Windows)

FIGURE 3.27
Select Import Folder (Add to Evernote)
(Windows)

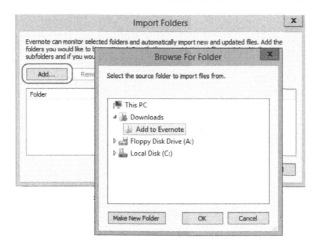

FIGURE 3.28
Import Folder Settings > Delete Files after Import

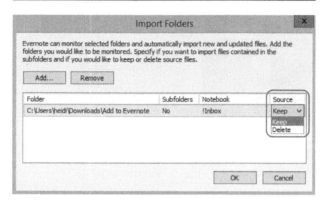

Saving Content from the Web

The Web Clipper is, arguably, one of Evernote's foremost features. With the Web Clipper, you can save articles, text, and images from the web directly into Evernote. The Web Clipper works with computers, mobile platforms, and most web browsers. As a lawyer, you might use the Web Clipper to clip articles or case law for later reading or reference.

Using the Web Clipper is simple. First, download the extension for your web browser at https://evernote.com/webclipper/. Web Clipper is available for Chrome, Safari, Internet Explorer 7+, Firefox, and Opera. Then, click on the extension in your browser to sign into Evernote and begin using. The Web Clipper for Safari is shown in Figure 3.29.

Clip and File a Web Page

When saving a web page, click the Web Clipper from your browser bar and a formatting box will appear on the right-hand side of the web page (see Figure 3.29). Here are a few options you'll use:

- Title: Ensure that the clip is titled. Evernote predicts a title based on the web page. You can edit that title directly in the title field.

- Organize: Select which notebook to save in. If you use tags, add a tag from this field. Only existing Evernote tags may be used. You can also add a remark to your note, which will appear at the top of the note immediately above a horizontal line that separates the remark from the web clip.

FIGURE 3.29
Web Clipper for Safari

Clip Formats

When saving a web page, click the Web Clipper and select the format you'd like to save in. Formats include the following:

- Article: Article format saves much of the content on the page, excluding headers, footers, advertisements, and other extraneous materials. You can expand or contract the article section to capture more or less of the content.
- Simplified article: This version takes the content from the article format and strips it down further to only the text and embedded media.
- Full page: As titled, full page saves the entire web page.
- PDF: When visiting a PDF on the web, saving the page as a PDF preserves its formatting.

- Bookmark: Saving as a Bookmark extracts only the website address and a few sentences of text (if available) as a page description.
- Screenshot: Selecting Screenshot allows you to take a snapshot of all or part of the browser screen. Drag and release to capture the section you desire.

Annotate a Clip

The Web Clipper provides several annotation tools. You can use the highlighter, immediately available when text appears on the web page, to highlight words or sections; or you can select Screenshot and use the annotation tools to mark it up before saving (see Figure 3.30).

FIGURE 3.30
Annotate a Web Clip via Screenshot Selection

Share a Clip

After saving a clip, you can use the Web Clipper to immediately share your clip via social media, e-mail, or copy the link into another program (see Figure 3.31).

FIGURE 3.31
Share Web Clip

POWER USER TIP

Customize your Web Clipper in Options, found at the bottom of the Web Clipper formatting box (see Figure 3.32). Turn on Evernote's smart filing feature to predict the proper notebook and tags based on your clipping and filing history. You can also view and set keyboard shortcuts for quickly opening the Web Clipper, previewing a clip, e-mailing a clip, annotating a clip, and more.

FIGURE 3.32
Access
Web Clipper
Options Menu

Saving Content via E-mail

You can save e-mails to Evernote in a few ways.

The most direct option is available only for Evernote Plus and Premium users (Basic users can try it out five times). With an assigned Evernote account e-mail address, you can send or forward any e-mail (including those with attachments) to Evernote. The e-mail subject line will become the note title, and the body of the e-mail will become the body of the note. You can find your assigned e-mail account by accessing your account via Evernote for web (sign in via www.evernote.com) and navigating to your Account Summary page (via Settings; see Figure 3.33). Your e-mail address will appear under Email Notes to (see Figure 3.34). Windows users can also find their assigned account e-mail address by clicking on Tools from the application menu and then on Account Info (see Figure 3.35). If you are a Premium user, you can customize your Evernote e-mail address. For efficiency, add your Evernote e-mail address to your electronic address book.

FIGURE 3.33
Access Account Settings (Web)

FIGURE 3.34
Find Your Evernote E-mail Address (Web)

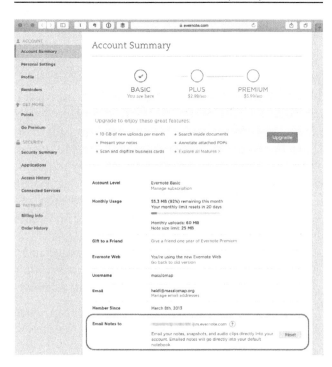

FIGURE 3.35
Find Your Evernote E-mail
Address (Windows)

If you do not have a Plus or Premium account, there are free workarounds to save e-mails from Gmail or Outlook for Windows.

Gmail: First you'll need to install the Web Clipper in your browser of choice. To save a Gmail message, open the message and select the Web Clipper. An option to save the e-mail will appear. If you have a Gmail conversation open, you can also select which messages in that conversation you'd like to save. Figure 3.36 displays the options for saving a Gmail message with the Web Clipper.

FIGURE 3.36
Save Gmail Message with Web Clipper

Outlook: When you install Evernote for Windows on your desktop, Evernote automatically installs an add-on to Microsoft Outlook (versions 2010 and 2013). You'll find a Save to Evernote button in the Outlook ribbon. Click on that button, and you can choose which notebook to save in, as well as add tags and remarks (that precede the note content). Figure 3.37 demonstrates how this add-on works.

FIGURE 3.37

Save Outlook Message with Evernote Add-On

POWER USER TIPS

You can apply the following power actions when capturing notes using your assigned Evernote account e-mail address.

1. Specify Notebook and Add Attributes. If not specified, your e-mailed note is saved to your default notebook. You can specify a notebook by adding @ plus the name of an existing notebook in the subject line after the subject (i.e., note title). To add tags, use # plus an existing tag following the notebook designation. To set a reminder, add the exclamation mark (!) plus a date in the year/month/day format (YYYY/MM/DD) immediately after the subject/note title.

   For example, using the following e-mail subject line

   Response to Motion !2016/01/15 @Case File XYZ #response #state court

   results in a note entitled Response to Motion with a reminder for January 15, 2016, in the notebook Case File XYZ with tags response and state court.

2. Append to an Existing Note. You can also insert + at the end of a subject line to append the content of an e-mail to an existing note. Evernote will append the body of the e-mail to the most recent note with the title as provided in the subject line of the e-mail.

For example, using the following e-mail subject line

Blog Post Ideas +

will append the body of the e-mail message to the end of the most recent note entitled Blog Post Ideas.

3. Auto-Filing. Rather than designate a specific notebook and attributes, Evernote's auto-filing feature predicts the note-book and tags by evaluating similar notes and then files the note accordingly. To turn on auto-file, go to your web account and then select Settings and Personal Settings. Check the box to turn on auto-filing.

3.4 Scanning to Evernote

Earlier in this chapter, you learned how to save content from your computer to Evernote by dragging and dropping files, using the attachment feature, e-mail, print to PDF (Mac), and import folders (Windows). Another simple way to get content into Evernote is by using your mobile device to snap a photo of a document or image. The Evernote app for smartphones provides an option to create a note from a photo (see Chapter 4 for more tips on using a mobile device). The app automatically finds the document in the frame and then rotates, crops, and adjusts the image before saving it directly to Evernote. Yet another option for scanning documents or images to Evernote is Evernote's iOS app, Scannable, which is similar to the native Evernote mobile app but has the added option of saving as a PDF or image, thereby allowing you to scan multipage PDFs.

For high-volume and more frequent scanning, Evernote also integrates with a variety of physical scanners. Certain brands of scanners, such as Fujitsu, Neat Connect, Canon, Doxie, Lexmark, and Brother, allow for direct scanning to Evernote. Evernote has also teamed up with Fujitsu to offer an Evernote Edition of the popular ScanSnap model by Fujitsu. The Evernote Edition provides extra features that other scanners don't, such as automatic recognition and filing of documents, receipts, photos, and business cards. It also comes with an Evernote Premium subscription for one year. The one significant caveat is that the Evernote Edition is compatible only with Evernote and will not scan directly to a computer hard drive (or any other application).

POWER USER TIP

You can replicate the Fujitsu ScanSnap Evernote Edition's direct scan to Evernote as described earlier with any scanner by automating the process with Windows import folders (discussed in Section 3.3) or Mac's Automator application. When you scan directly to a Windows import folder, that file or files will automatically go to Evernote. On the Mac, you'll need to use Automator, a native system program. Open Automator and create a new Folder Action. Indicate which desktop folder you'd like to import from (i.e., Evernote Import Folder) and then add an AppleScript to pull your files from that folder and place them in Evernote. For step-by-step instructions, take a look at this video by Brooks Duncan: www.documentsnap.com/evernote-mac-import-folder.

3.5 Naming Conventions and Organization

The key to any paperless system is thoughtful organization and consistency. Without these two elements, you cannot expect to reliably access your data when you need it, which in turn defeats the entire purpose of the system. To get the most out of your use of Evernote, you'll need to design a notebook and stack structure, as well as set a naming convention protocol for your notes and tags.

Notebooks and Stacks

When viewed in your sidebar, stacks are organized alphabetically and notebooks within the notebook stacks are also organized alphabetically by their title. (For other sorting options—date updated and note count—click on the Notebooks icon to view all notebooks in the main panel.) Within this sorting system, special characters will sort first, then numbers (chronologically), and then letters. Therefore, your system must take that process into consideration. For example, if you use Evernote for both business and personal purposes, you might use the prefix W (for work) and P (for personal) to identify those respective stacks. That way, all your work and personal notebook stacks will be grouped together. For further organization, you could promote those stacks above others by enclosing the W and P in parentheses. This works just like renaming your default notebook to !Inbox (see Section 3.2). Using parentheses will sort your work and personal stacks before other alphanumeric stacks.

Here is one example of how you can use prefixes to tailor the organization of your notebooks/stacks:

!Inbox
(P) House
(P) Important Documents
(P) Receipts
(W) Firm Administration
(W) Legal Research
(W) Marketing
Read Later

Next, think about how you'd like to organize your notebooks within your stacks. To create a specific order, you can use a numeric system that might look like this:

(W) Firm Administration
    01 Office and Systems Information
    02 Policies and Procedures
    03 Financial Management
    04 Forms and Templates
    05 CLE
    06 Meetings
    07 Travel

POWER USER TIP

If you use special characters to manually sort your notebooks and stacks, be aware that Evernote sorts characters differently depending on the platform used. For example, Evernote Windows will sort #Inbox before (W) Firm Administration. However, on Evernote Mac, (W) Firm Administration will appear before #Inbox. If you use multiple platforms, the best way to ensure consistency is to use numeric prefixes rather than special characters.

Notes and Tags

Notes and tags also follow the default sorting system by note title—first special characters, then numerals, then letters. Notes can also be sorted by date created, date updated, source URL, and size.

A best practice for creating any paperless filing system is to begin your document title with the year, month, and day format (YYYYMMDD) to create a chronological record of your files. The same concept applies to Evernote notes. The year, month, and day format could be designated as follows:

20150901
2015-09-01
2015.09.01
2015_09_01

Use whatever date format you prefer. As long as you are consistent with your date format, your notes will be sorted in chronological order. Next, determine how you'll name whatever comes after the date. For a letter from opposing counsel, you might use the following structure: `[DATE] Ltr fr [OPPOSING COUNSEL] re [DESCRIPTION]`. In this format, a letter from Perry Mason on September 1, 2015, regarding a settlement offer would be entitled as follows: `2015-09-01 Ltr fr P. Mason re settlement offer`. This format works well for those who rely heavily on the notebook structure and note lists.

Titling notes by date works well for certain notes, such as invoices, fee agreements, and letters, but might not be appropriate for other notes, such as legal research, office information, and templates. Again, consistency is key. Determine which documents need a date and which do not. Set a uniform naming convention for both.

Naming of tags follows the same mantra as note conventions; consistency is key. Consider which categories of notes would be helpful to track. For example, using the tag `p.mason` for all correspondence to and from Perry Mason allows you to pull up all that correspondence with a click of a button. If you abbreviate counsel's first name and use the full last name (i.e., `p.mason`), then that should remain your convention for all name tags. Tags are not commonly viewed in list format, and thus the sorting order shouldn't matter in most situations. But, if you'd like your tags organized in a certain way, you'll need to use prefixes as described earlier for labeling notebooks and notebook stacks. For example, if you use tags to identify your to-do items, which could carry across notebooks (as discussed in Section 5.5), you might want that tag to appear at the top of your tag list (alternatively, you could create a shortcut for that tag, as described in Section 3.8). For example, you could tag priority to-do items as !Priority so that the category appears at the top of your tag list in the sidebar.

POWER USER TIP

An alternative form of titling notes for those who rely primarily on Evernote's search features (discussed further in Section 3.7) is to keep the title simple and use tags and other note attributes to identify the note. Here is a sample format: Ltr re [DESCRIPTION] + tag [OPPOSING COUNSEL]. Applying this naming convention to the above example, the title would appear as Ltr re settlement offer and be tagged p.mason. To set the appropriate date, navigate to the note's information and change the date created accordingly, as shown in Figure 3.38. Not only can you quickly find this note via a search, but you have additional options. For example, you can search for all correspondence from Perry Mason between certain dates by using search syntax for tags, date created, and text (Ltr).

FIGURE 3.38
Using Note Attributes

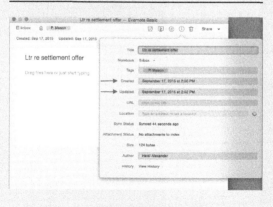

3.6 Sharing and Collaborating

Once you've added content to your notes and notebooks, you can start sharing that content and collaborating with others in a number of ways. Notes, as well as entire notebooks, may be shared with Evernote users and nonusers alike. Sharing may take the form of a static note sent via e-mail or a dynamic note or notebook for collaboration purposes. Evernote even has a dedicated feature to facilitate sharing and collaborating with others, called work chat. Clicking on the work chat icon in the sidebar opens a communication portal from within the Evernote platform, thus allowing for more efficient work on shared content.

Sharing Public Web Notes and Notebooks

Share notes and notebooks with others for viewing purposes by creating a public sharing link. Evernote generates a unique web link for that note or notebook. Anyone (including non–Evernote users) with that link can view the note. Evernote users can save the note into their own workspace. When you share via a public link, any subsequent edits or additions that you make to your note will be available to your viewer in real time as you sync your account. You can stop sharing the public link with the click of a button. Of course, public note and notebook sharing would not be an appropriate means of sharing confidential information.

Share a Public Note Link

Mac

For Mac users, to create a public note link, first click on the triangle beside the Share button (see Figure 3.39). Then, select Copy Public Link (see Figure 3.40). The link is now copied to your desktop clipboard, and you can paste it anywhere you like.

FIGURE 3.39	**FIGURE 3.40**
Create a Public Link (Mac)	Copy a Public Link (Mac)

Share Note...
Share Notebook...

Post Public Link To ▶
Copy Public Link
Stop Sharing Public Link

Manage Note Permissions...
Manage Notebook Permissions...

Windows

The process is similar for Windows users, except that you will select Copy Share URL (see Figure 3.41).

Anyone with access to this link can view the note from a web browser and save it to their own Evernote accounts (see Figure 3.42).

FIGURE 3.41
Create and Copy a Public Link
(Windows)

FIGURE 3.42
Shared Note via Web Browser

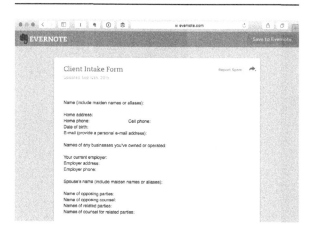

Stop Sharing a Public Link

Mac

To stop sharing a public note link on a Mac, click on the triangle beside the Share button and then select Stop Sharing Public Link (see Figure 3.43).

FIGURE 3.43
Stop Public Note Sharing (Mac)

Windows

To stop sharing a public note link on Windows, click on the triangle beside the Share button and then select Modify Sharing (see Figure 3.44). To stop sharing the link, uncheck the box next to "Enable public link (see Figure 3.45).

FIGURE 3.44
Modify Sharing (Windows)

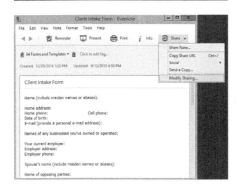

FIGURE 3.45
Stop Sharing Public Note Link (Windows)

FIGURE 3.46
Select Notebook and Publish (Mac)

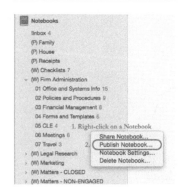

Share a Public Notebook Link

Mac

To create a public link for a notebook on the Mac, right-click on the notebook you'd like to share, then select Publish Notebook (see Figure 3.46). Next, click Publish (see Figure 3.47). The public link will appear. You can also delete the public link from this screen (see Figure 3.48).

FIGURE 3.47
Publish Public Link (Mac)

FIGURE 3.48
Access to Public Link and Removal of Public Link (Mac)

Windows

The process is similar for sharing a public notebook link via Windows desktop. First, right-click on the notebook you'd like to share, then select Modify Sharing (see Figure 3.49). Next, click Publish (see Figure 3.50). The public link will appear with an option to delete it (see Figure 3.51).

FIGURE 3.49
Select Notebook and Modify Sharing (Windows)

FIGURE 3.50
Publish Public Link (Windows)

FIGURE 3.51
Access to Public Link and Removal of Public Link (Windows)

Anyone with access to this link can view the notebook contents and join the notebook from their own Evernote account (see Figure 3.52).

FIGURE 3.52
Shared Notebook via Web Browser

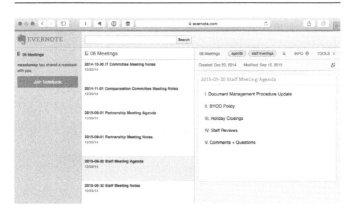

POWER USER TIP

You can use the public sharing link to create links to your Evernote notes/notebooks from other programs. This link can be quite helpful if you use a separate task manager program, such as Wunderlist. To link to a particular Evernote note from Wunderlist, merely insert the public sharing link (see Figure 3.53).

FIGURE 3.53
Public Link to Evernote Notebook
from Wunderlist

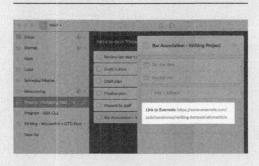

Sharing by E-mail

Share a copy of your note or multiple notes with others via e-mail. The recipient (who need not be an Evernote user) receives a copy of the note in the body of the e-mail. Unlike web sharing, the e-mail contains only a snapshot of the note; it will not reflect any changes that you make after you've sent the note.

Mac

To e-mail a copy of a note from the Mac desktop application, click on the note you'd like to e-mail, then select Note from the application menu. Next, click on More Sharing and then on Email a Copy (see Figure 3.54). Then you can complete and send the e-mail (see Figure 3.55).

FIGURE 3.54
E-mail a Copy of the Note (Mac)

FIGURE 3.55
Send the E-mail (Mac)

Windows

You can e-mail a copy of the note from the Windows desktop application right from the Share button within the note (similar to creating public note links). Click the triangle beside the Share button, then select Send a Copy (see Figure 3.56). You'll then complete and send the e-mail, as indicated in Figure 3.55.

FIGURE 3.56
Send a Copy of the Note
(Windows)

The e-mail will appear to the recipient as shown in Figure 3.57.

FIGURE 3.57
Recipient View

Share within Evernote

Share notes and notebooks with other Evernote users for viewing and editing by using Evernote's work chat feature. Work chat is a messaging tool in Evernote that can be used to communicate and collaborate with other Evernote users.

With work chat, you can share individual notes with other Evernote users via the Share button (see Figure 3.58). Type in a contact name or e-mail address to share.

FIGURE 3.58

Share via Work Chat

Once a note is shared, all changes made by shared users of the note will appear in each user's respective workspace. To collaborate further, you can also share entire notebooks with other Evernote users. When you share an entire notebook with another Evernote user, that notebook becomes part of that user's workspace.

You can set and change note and notebook user sharing permissions to view only, edit, or edit and invite (for inviting others to view and edit the note or notebook). You can also stop sharing the note or notebook by modifying the permissions.

Mac

Mac desktop users can access sharing permissions for notes and notebooks by clicking on the triangle beside the Share button in an individual note (see Figure 3.59). You can also access sharing permissions for notebooks by right-clicking on a notebook, then selecting Modify Sharing (see Figure 3.60). Setting different permissions is shown in Figure 3.61.

FIGURE 3.59
Access Sharing Permissions—
Note/Notebooks (Mac)

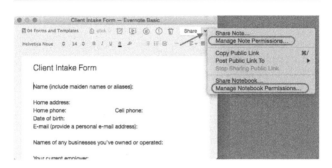

FIGURE 3.60
Access Sharing
Permissions—
Notebooks (Mac)

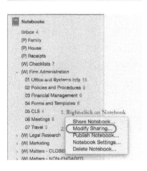

FIGURE 3.61
Setting Permissions—Mac

Windows

Windows desktop users can access sharing permissions by a process similar to the one for Mac users. Click on the triangle beside the Share button in an individual note and then select Modify Sharing (see Figure 3.62). For notebooks, right-click on the notebook, then click on Modify Sharing (see Figure 3.63).

FIGURE 3.62
Access Sharing Permissions—
Note (Windows)

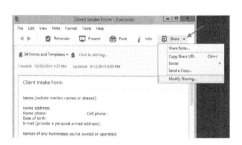

FIGURE 3.63
Access Sharing Permissions—
Notebook (Windows)

3.7 Searching with Evernote

Search is one of Evernote's most valuable features. Nearly everything in Evernote is searchable, making it easy to pinpoint information with the click of a button and difficult to lose track of information you've saved. Search includes the contents of notes, tags, attachments, images and PDFs, and even handwritten notes. As discussed previously, you are limited to a certain number of notebooks; thus, there's a limit to how far you can rely on notebooks and stacks for organization. This makes search an attractive way to further sort and find content.

For searching within images and PDFs, Evernote has what's called optical character recognition (OCR) as a built-in component of the software. OCR allows Evernote to find text, whether it's typewritten or handwritten. It can even decipher text written at a 90-degree or 270-degree vertical orientation. To search for text within an image, it must first be uploaded to Evernote and then processed with OCR by Evernote's servers. As a result, OCR can be used only for notes saved in synchronized notebooks. For Basic and Plus users, this process may take a few minutes, whereas Premium users get bumped to the top of the server queue.

For OCR to work on PDFs, a number of requirements must be met:

- Must contain typed text (Tip: For handwritten notes, scan as an image, not as a PDF.)
- Must not contain text that you can select or copy
- Must contain at least 1025 pixels of data
- Must be less than 100 pages
- Must be less than 25 megabytes

- Must not be password protected, corrupted, or unreadable

Basic and Plus accounts provide OCR only for image files. Thus, you cannot use a Basic or Plus account to search image-based/scanned PDFs, office documents, or attachments to a note. However, if you convert an office document (with text) to a PDF and then save it to Evernote, your Basic or Plus account will provide OCR in that document.

Using the search bar in the Evernote desktop toolbar, you can conduct simple and complex searches, and you can save searches for future use. When beginning a search, you'll see a drop-down menu with the location of your search, recent searches, saved searches, and option to further tailor your search.

Global Search

To search across all content, simply type in the text you are looking for, as demonstrated in Figure 3.64. The resulting list of notes will display all notes that contain the text, with highlights to each portion of the note in which the text appears.

FIGURE 3.64
Conduct a Global Search

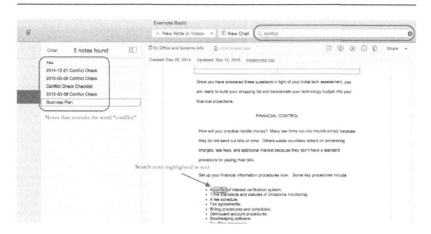

Searching within Specific Notes and Notebooks

The simplest way to search for content within a particular note is to open the note and then use a shortcut to pull up the search bar: ⌘F for Mac and Ctrl + F for Windows. To search within a particular notebook on the Mac, click in the search bar and a drop-down menu of options will appear (see Figure 3.65). At the bottom of the menu, select Add Search Option, then select Notebook, and then specify the notebook you'd like to search. See Figure 3.66 (Mac) and Figure 3.67 (Windows). A second

FIGURE 3.65
Add Search Option (Mac)

FIGURE 3.66
Select Notebook from
Add Search Option (Mac)

FIGURE 3.67
Select Individual
Notebook and Add (Mac)

way is to open the notebook you'd like to search first and then conduct your search. For Windows users, first you'll need to click the magnifying glass icon on the left-hand side of the search bar and then select Search Current Content (see Figure 3.68). Next, from your Notebook List, select the notebook you'd like to search within and then type in your search term (see Figure 3.69).

Another and more efficient way to search within a note or notebook is by using operators to conduct your search. Turn to the end of this section for a listing of popular operators.

FIGURE 3.68
Search Current Content (Windows)

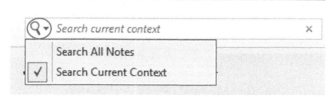

FIGURE 3.69
Select Notebook (Windows)

Searching Tags

If you have used tags to further organize your notes, you'll likely need to search for notes labeled with certain tags. To do this, use the operator tag:[insert name of tag]. For tags with multiple words, place the tag name within quotes. For example, tag:"Evernote Book".

Saving Searches

Is there a particular search that you conduct frequently and thus would like to save for future use? For example, (1) as you prepare for a deposition, you might often need to view all notes tagged deposition materials within a certain client's notebook; or (2) for reporting travel expenses, you might often need access to all notes tagged travel expenses.

Mac desktop users can save searches by first conducting the search from the search bar, then navigating to Edit on the application menu and then clicking on Find and selecting Save Search (see Figure 3.70). Then, rename your search.

FIGURE 3.70
Save Search (Mac)

For Windows desktop users, conduct your search, then select Save Search under the search bar (see Figure 3.71) or New Saved Search from the application menu under File (see Figure 3.72). Then, rename your search. When you click in the search bar (Mac or Windows), your new saved search will show below.

FIGURE 3.71
Save Search via Search Bar (Windows)

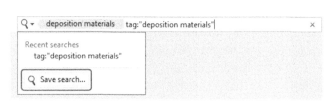

FIGURE 3.72
Save Search via Application Menu (Windows)

File	Edit	View	Note	Format	Tools	Help	
New Note						Ctrl+N	
New Chat						Ctrl+Alt+C	
New Tag...						Ctrl+Shift+T	
New Notebook							▶
New Saved Search...							

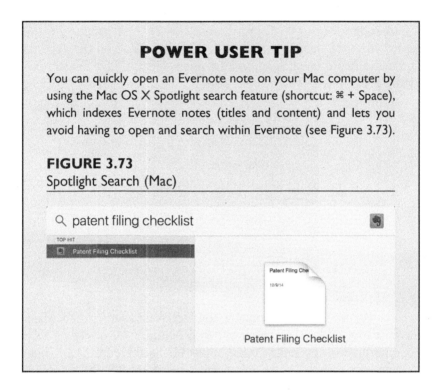

POWER USER TIP

You can quickly open an Evernote note on your Mac computer by using the Mac OS X Spotlight search feature (shortcut: ⌘ + Space), which indexes Evernote notes (titles and content) and lets you avoid having to open and search within Evernote (see Figure 3.73).

FIGURE 3.73
Spotlight Search (Mac)

Descriptive Search

The descriptive search feature is available for Mac desktop only. Rather than pinpointing the precise text, tags, or notes you are looking for, you can use natural language to describe the search. For example, if you are looking for all notes you created yesterday, type "notes created yesterday," and Evernote will return results of all the notes you created yesterday, as shown in Figure 3.74. Descriptive search works particularly well for complex searches to avoid stringing together a bunch of operators to make it happen. For example, type: "reminders due in the next month and tagged marketing," and Evernote will list all the notes tagged marketing that also contain a reminder for the next month. Other available descriptive searches can result in notes that contain certain documents ("notes with attachments"), images ("notes with photos"), from a certain source, such as a web clip or e-mail ("web clips" or "e-mail"), to-do items ("incomplete tasks"), and more.

FIGURE 3.74
Descriptive Search (Mac)

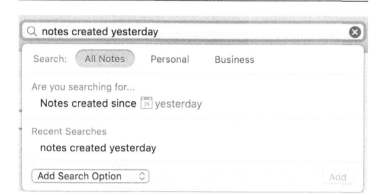

Operators and Complex Searches

Just like you would with a Lexis or Westlaw search, you can use Evernote to string together operators to conduct a complex search. Evernote provides a listing of all operators on its Help & Learning site, but here are some common ones you should know:

+ or -: Search with or without certain text.

*: Search for a variation of the text.

any: Search for any of the words, rather than all the words.

created [YYYY/MM/DD or day-1]: Search for notes created on or after a certain date (YYYY/MM/DD). Or, search on some date prior to today (day-1).

encryption: Search for encrypted notes.

intitle: Search within a note's title.

notebook: Search within a particular notebook.

"..." (quotation marks): Search for the exact words.

source [mail.smtp or web.clip or mobile.*]: Search by the source that added the note (i.e., e-mail, web clip, or mobile device)

tag: Search for a specific tag or tags.

todo: Search for notes with checkboxes. Use todo:true for notes containing checked checkboxes and todo:false for notes containing unchecked checkboxes.

POWER USER TIP

You can build more complex searches by pairing some of the operators. For example, to find notes within your Firm Administration notebook created on or after 1/1/15 that have incomplete to-dos, and contain the word "finance":

notebook:"Firm Administration" created:20150101
todo:false +finance

3.8 Customizing Your Workspace

To get the most out of Evernote, you'll want to customize your workspace. You can set shortcuts for frequently used notebooks and tags, organize your toolbar, adjust sidebar content, set viewing panes, and more.

Sidebar

The sidebar appears on the left-hand side of your workspace. From there, you can access much of your Evernote content. To configure what you see in the sidebar, open View in your application menu, then select Sidebar Options (Mac), see Figure 3.75, or "Left Panel" (Windows), see Figure 3.76. You can choose what to show in the sidebar, including work chat, shortcuts, recent notes (Mac only), notes, notebooks, tags, atlas, market, upgrade, and announcements. You likely don't need all of these options available every day in your sidebar. Instead, include only the content sections that you access often.

Customize your sidebar further by setting shortcuts for frequently used notebooks, notes, tags, and Searches. For example, you might add a shortcut for your default notebook. To add a note shortcut, right-click on the note and select Add to Shortcuts.

For Mac users, to add a notebook/stack or tag shortcut, you must do so within the notebook or tag view rather than from the sidebar. Go to that view and right-click on the notebook/stack or tag to add

FIGURE 3.75
Sidebar Options (Mac)

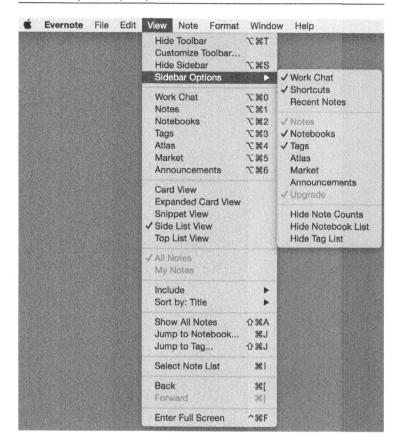

FIGURE 3.76
Sidebar Options (Windows)

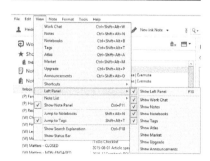

FIGURE 3.77
Add Notebook Shortcuts (Mac)

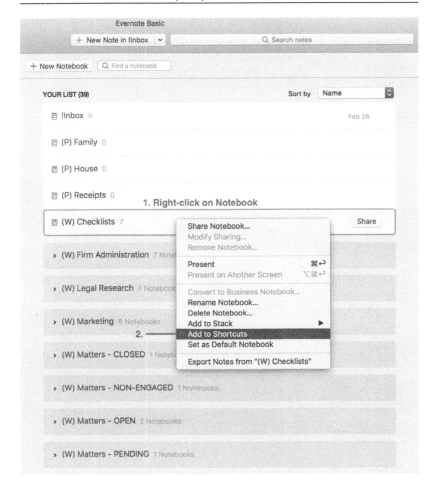

the shortcut (see Figure 3.77). For Windows users, right-click on a notebook/stack or tag from your sidebar and select Add to Shortcuts (see Figure 3.78).

To add a shortcut for a saved search, click on the search bar and find the saved search you'd like to add. Then drag and drop it in the Shortcuts section of the sidebar.

FIGURE 3.78
Add Notebook Shortcuts (Windows)

FIGURE 3.79
Sidebar Configuration Example

You can configure your sidebar in many ways. Figure 3.79 demonstrates one possible configuration, which displays work chat, shortcuts, notes, the notebook list, and the tag list.

Evernote Menu

Your Evernote menu is the toolbar that appears above the sidebar and notes. You can customize it by adding or removing tools such as buttons to create a new note or new chat, show recent account activity, or search notes. Currently, the Windows desktop client allows for more configuration options (E-mail, Copy URL, Delete, and others) than does the Mac client.

Mac

To configure the Evernote menu on the Mac, go to the View menu and select Customize Toolbar from the application menu. You can then add or remove the tools you'd like on your Evernote menu, as shown in Figure 3.80.

FIGURE 3.80
Toolbar Configuration Options (Mac)

Windows

To configure the Evernote menu on Windows, go to the Tools menu and select Customize Toolbar from the application menu. Then add or remove the tools you'd like on your Evernote menu, as shown in Figure 3.81.

FIGURE 3.81
Toolbar Configuration Options (Windows)

Notes

Notes appear to the right of the sidebar. A variety of viewing and sorting configurations are available for notes. See Figure 3.82 (Mac) and Figure 3.83 (Windows). Viewing options is a matter of each user's aesthetics and is based on the amount of information you'd like available. In the Note List view, you'll get a simplified list of note titles that make up whatever shortcut, notebook, tag, or search you've chosen. In the Snippets view, you'll see the note title as well as the first few lines of text or image thumbnail. In the Card view, you'll see a larger view of the note along with the title, initial text, or image. The List view will always allow you to view more notes in the list because the view doesn't include extra content. You can configure the List, Snippets, or Card views to

FIGURE 3.82
Note Configuration Options (Mac)

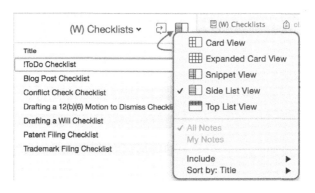

FIGURE 3.83
Note Configuration Options (Windows)

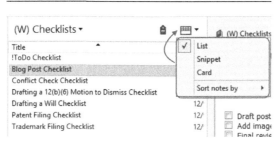

appear to the left-hand side or above the note. Within the List and Card views, you have a number of further sorting options: by title, date created or updated, source URL, and size. If you use naming conventions consisting of date first (discussed in Section 3.5), then sorting by title is your best option.

POWER USER TIP

Reorganize your shortcuts by dragging and dropping to move a shortcut up or down the list.

Evernote on the Go

Evernote can be accessed from any mobile device through a web browser. In addition, Evernote has developed applications for a variety of popular mobile platforms including smartphones, tablets, and wearables. For Apple users, you can download Evernote in the App Store on iTunes to your iPhone, iPad, iPod Touch, and Apple Watch. For Android users, you can download Evernote from Google Play to your smartphone, tablet, and Android Wear smartwatch. For Windows users, you can download Evernote from the Windows App Store to your Windows phone and Evernote Touch for your Windows 8 and 10 touchscreen device. Evernote users running Windows 8 and 10 touchscreen devices can use either the Evernote Touch app or the full desktop app. The Evernote Touch app maximizes the touchscreen capabilities. Evernote also makes an application for Blackberry 10 users via BlackBerry World.

Evernote conforms to each platform's operating system, thus assimilating to the look, feel, and functionality of each device. Evernote's basic features, such as creating or editing a note, searching notes, and sharing notes, will be available from any device. Evernote provides instructions for each platform via https://evernote.com /evernote/guide.

The next two sections present a handful of tips for using two popular mobile platforms: Android and iOS.

4.1 Top Tips for Android Platform

- Download the Evernote App from Google Play. From the widget on your home screen or lock screen, you can quickly create a note or save content.
- Take handwritten notes using your finger or a stylus directly from your note. Tap the Add Handwriting button (paper and pen icon) to start writing.
- Clip web pages to Evernote by navigating to the options menu from your device's web browser, clicking on Share and then Add to Evernote. Tap the Elephant button to designate a notebook and tags.
- Attach files or photos to your note by clicking the + button from within the note or note list and selecting the file or photo from your device.
- Use the camera to scan documents and images by clicking the + button to create a new note from the camera or add to an existing note. Use the business card camera option to scan business cards. Evernote will automatically parse the name, company, addresses, and telephone number and then prompt you to save it to your contacts.
- Turn on the auto-title feature from Settings > Note Creation > Enable Auto-Title. When you create a new note, Evernote predicts a title based on the time the note was created and the content of the note. This feature helps you to quickly save and find the note later.

4.2 Top Tips for iOS Platform

- Use Evernote's Scannable application from the App Store on iTunes to scan documents to Evernote. Scannable automatically identifies the type of document—receipt, document, photo, or business card—and will focus, adjust, enhance, and crop the image. It also works to scan and compile multipage documents. With Scannable, you can save business cards into Evernote and to your device contacts, and supplement them with information from LinkedIn. After scanning a business card and adding a contact, you can choose to send that individual your contact information. Although it's an Evernote app, it also provides for actions outside of Evernote such as mailing and messaging as well as saving to iCloud and other cloud services.

- Save web pages from Safari with the iOS share extension. To activate Evernote's share extension, in Safari, click on the Share button and then click on More. Turn on the button for Evernote. Now you can use the Share button and then click on the Evernote icon to save a web page to Evernote and designate a notebook.

- Add the Evernote widget to the Today view in your Notification Center by swiping down from the top of the screen, clicking on Today, then scrolling down to Edit. When accessed from the Today view, the Evernote widget gives you a quick way to create a new note or new work chat. It will also display titles and a summary from your frequently viewed, recently viewed, and recently updated notes.

- Turn on Suggested Note Titles from Settings > General > Suggested Note Titles. When you create a new note, Evernote predicts a title based on your calendar events, your location, and note contents. This works well for on-the-spot meeting notes, allowing you to quickly start and save a note and easily find it later.

4.3 A Word about Wearables

If you've jumped on the wearables bandwagon, you'll be happy to know that Evernote has developed apps for Apple Watch and Android Wear. While these apps won't have full functionality, you can receive notifications, create notes, check off to-dos, and search using voice command. In line with the smart capabilities, these wearable apps can also reveal notes created near your location and those recently viewed on any platform.

Evernote in Your Law Practice

Now that you have a sense of what Evernote can do and how to use it, this chapter provides suggestions for applying Evernote to your law practice. Indeed, you can use Evernote in a variety of ways. The following ideas represent the most popular uses among lawyers and should provide a guide to tailor Evernote to your own office. Treat Evernote as you would any other office system or process; map out how it will integrate into your workflow; design a process (consistency is key), test it, implement it, and continue to refine it. As with any new system, there will be a learning curve, but in the end you'll find yourself with a more productive and efficient law practice.

There are four primary categories of Evernote use by lawyers: firm administration, case management, legal research, and marketing. Among those categories, there could be limitless subcategories. The following material identifies the most common uses within those categories. As a bonus, included is a time management section with suggestions for using checklists, storing reading material, and implementing strategies such as Getting Things Done® (GTD®).

These suggestions for organizing your legal work follow the naming conventions and organization discussed in Section 3.5. If you use your Evernote workspace for both personal and business purposes, I suggest using the (P) and (W) prefixes, also as explained in Section 3.5.

For each of the four primary categories, I suggest using notebooks and notebook stacks. Most lawyers I know are more comfortable organizing their workspaces this way; to a degree, it's analogous to an electronic filing system (folders containing folders containing documents). Some would argue that the most enlightened Evernote user would organize by tags rather than notebooks, again due to the limit on the number of Evernote notebooks and the power of Evernote's search feature. You'll see examples of this method used by my featured lawyers (see Chapter 7).

Ask yourself, are you someone who uses search functionality to access documents from your computer? Or, do you navigate to a certain folder and expect to find the document there? The latter is still more common and more comfortable for most lawyers, while the former may prove to be more efficient in Evernote. But, of course, do what works for you!

5.1 Firm Administration

Think about what information you need to administer and manage your practice. That's what you'd store in the Firm Administration stack. First, create a notebook stack and label it Firm Administration. Now, what categories fall into Firm Administration? Those categories then become your notebooks within the stack. To get you started, Figure 5.1 as discussed in the following segment provides a sampling of information you might include in your Firm Administration notebook.

FIGURE 5.1

Firm Administration
Stack Example

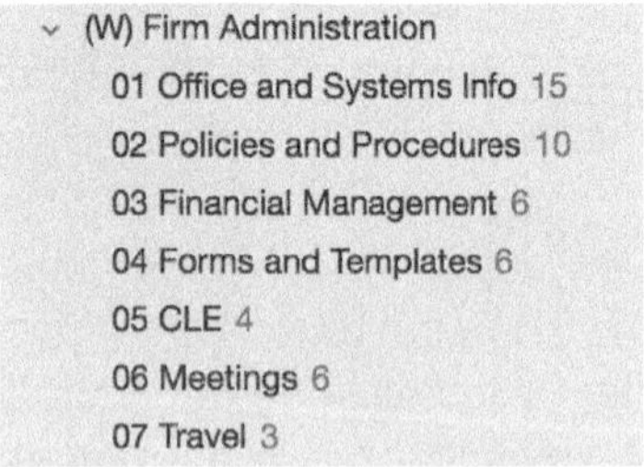

ˇ (W) Firm Administration
   01 Office and Systems Info 15
   02 Policies and Procedures 10
   03 Financial Management 6
   04 Forms and Templates 6
   05 CLE 4
   06 Meetings 6
   07 Travel 3

Office and Systems Information

Store information related to your office and systems, such as your bank accounts; FedEx and UPS accounts; data backups and storage; Internet router and telephone; access to Internet sites like social media, website, and hosting; contact for IT support, accountant, and bookkeeper;

malpractice insurance information; software program licenses; lease documentation and contact for landlord; and office address, phone number, fax, and e-mail addresses. From a law practice management perspective, keeping this information in a central repository is essential for succession planning and preparing for any unforeseen circumstances. Create a new note for each of the subcategories just listed. Figure 5.2 provides a sample listing of notes that might appear in an Office and Systems Information notebook. For sensitive information, such as financial account numbers, you may want to encrypt that data using Evernote's encryption tool (discussed in Section 6.3).

FIGURE 5.2
Office and Systems Information Notebook Example

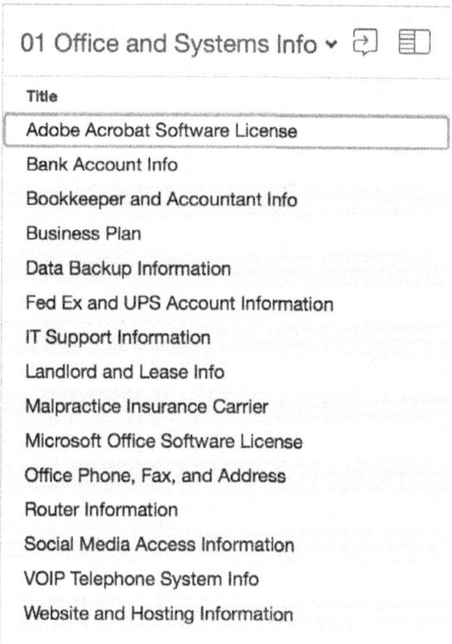

01 Office and Systems Info ∨ ⮂ ▤

Title

Adobe Acrobat Software License

Bank Account Info

Bookkeeper and Accountant Info

Business Plan

Data Backup Information

Fed Ex and UPS Account Information

IT Support Information

Landlord and Lease Info

Malpractice Insurance Carrier

Microsoft Office Software License

Office Phone, Fax, and Address

Router Information

Social Media Access Information

VOIP Telephone System Info

Website and Hosting Information

Policies and Procedures

Save policies and procedures for quick reference. Use Evernote's sharing features to circulate policies to staff and collaborate on drafts. A few note titles might include policies and processes for file management, trust accounting reconciliation, disaster recovery, retention and disposition, confidentiality, client intake, information security, and personnel, as shown in Figure 5.3.

FIGURE 5.3
Policies and Procedures Notebook Example

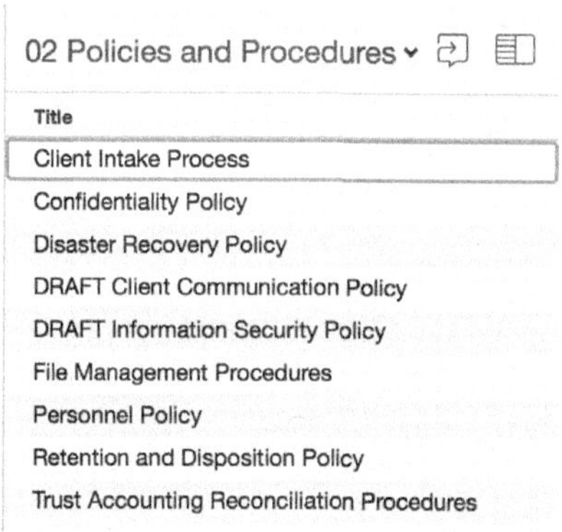

02 Policies and Procedures ∨ ⮂ ▤

Title

Client Intake Process

Confidentiality Policy

Disaster Recovery Policy

DRAFT Client Communication Policy

DRAFT Information Security Policy

File Management Procedures

Personnel Policy

Retention and Disposition Policy

Trust Accounting Reconciliation Procedures

Financial Management

Stop keeping paper copies of invoices and receipts, and instead upload them to your Evernote Financial Management notebook (see Figure 5.4) and discard the originals. You can scan, use Evernote's photo feature, or use Scannable (for iPhone) to snap a photo and save directly into your notebook of choice. To further sort and identify invoices and

FIGURE 5.4
Financial Management
Notebook Example

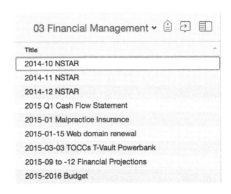

receipts, use tags that correspond to line items in your budget. For example, tag all Internet and electric bills utilities, invoices for supplies from Staples office supplies, and malpractice and other insurance premium invoices business insurance. You can also add text to the note with, for example, a memo to identify the purpose of the purchase, as shown in Figure 5.5. Your

FIGURE 5.5
Using Tags to Categorize Types of Receipts

Financial Management notebook can also serve as a repository for other important documents such as financial reports, statements, and budgets.

Forms and Templates

Do you have forms or templates that you use frequently in practice? Examples include client intake, closing letters, fee agreements, non-engagement letters, and practice-related forms such as purchase and sale agreements, corporate organizational documents, or litigation documents. Store them in your Forms and Templates notebook, as shown in Figure 5.6. When you'd like to use a form, duplicate it by copying it to a client notebook and inserting the individual matter information (see Figure 5.7).

You might also want to have a notebook for materials related to Continuing Legal Education (CLE). This notebook could be used to store announcements of upcoming programs clipped via web, sent via e-mail, or entered manually; lists of programs you've attended; certification of attendance forms; and materials for future reference,

FIGURE 5.6
Forms and Templates
Notebook Example

FIGURE 5.7
Copy a Note to Another Notebook

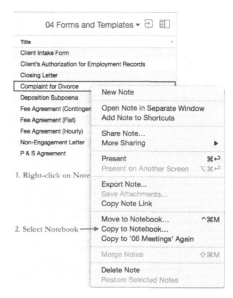

FIGURE 5.8
CLE Notebook Example

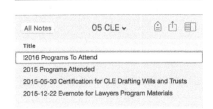

FIGURE 5.9
Using Tags to Categorize CLE Notes

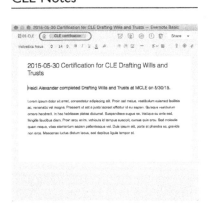

as shown in Figure 5.8. Use tags, such as CLE materials and CLE certification, to further categorize notes (see Figure 5.9) and then use a search to access them when needed.

Meetings

Save agendas and other materials for easy access during meetings and safekeeping (see Figure 5.10). Quickly open a new note and start taking notes at the meeting. Evernote automatically saves the note and syncs it to all your devices when you are connected to the Internet. If you later need to access that note, you can do so from any of your devices. Use Evernote's sharing tools to send the meeting notes to others or circulate an agenda and materials before the meeting. Use tags such as `partnership`, `staff`, `committee`, `agenda`, and `notes` to organize and find meeting materials by the type of meeting (see Figure 5.11).

FIGURE 5.10
Meeting Notebook Example

FIGURE 5.11
Using Tags to Categorize Meeting Notes

Travel

Prepare for business travel by keeping your travel documents, such as itineraries, airline tickets, and hotel confirmations, in a dedicated Travel notebook (see Figure 5.12). With Evernote's sharing features, you can keep others informed. Use this notebook as well to capture any notes en route.

FIGURE 5.12
Travel Notebook Example

All Notes	07 Travel ⌄	📤 📑

Title
2015-10-01 Hilton Confirmation
2015-10-01 United Airline Confirmation
2015-10-02 Itinerary - California re Meeting with Larry Page

5.2 Case Management

With all the aforementioned features—storage in a variety of formats, sync, collaboration, annotation, and search—Evernote can be a powerful case management tool. Some lawyers use Evernote as their primary case management database, while others use it to supplement a case management program designed for legal. Indeed, at least one case management system, Rocket Matter, provides a direct integration with Evernote (see the Integrations section in the appendix for more information about Rocket Matter and Evernote integration). Either approach to case management works, although the former will require some creativity, strong organization, and proper planning on your part. To help you envision a system—whether as your primary or supplemental case manager—this section provides you with some guidance. Remember, however, that there is no "right" way to organize your system. Do what works for you—just make sure to be consistent!

A word about security: Whenever we lawyers talk about storing client information electronically, we need to be cognizant of our ethical obligations to protect our client's data from unauthorized access. As mentioned previously, to get the most benefit from Evernote, you should use synchronized notebooks to store your data. This effectively means you are storing your data in the cloud via Evernote's servers. You could use local notebooks only to store your client data, thus keeping that data confined to your computer alone (requiring security measures taken on your own, which I argue cannot rival a major cloud service provider); but again, you'll lose much of

Evernote's functionality. As with any other cloud provider, you must do your own due diligence to determine whether you are comfortable storing your client's data using that service. Chapter 6 contains a security primer outlining Evernote's policies and history. Armed with that information and any updated terms of service or information (since the publishing of this book), you can make your own informed determination.

Setting Up Your System

As discussed in the section introduction, the most intuitive way for a lawyer to set up a case management system is to use stacks and notebooks as the primary means of organization, adding tags to further categorize content. First, set up notebook stacks for pending, open, closed, and non-engaged matters. Each stack will contain client notebooks labeled with their client identifiers, as shown by example in Figure 5.13. Your client identifier might start with the date the client signed the fee agreement and include initials (i.e., 2015-08-01 AleHe for client, Heidi Alexander, who signs a fee agreement on August 1, 2015), or start with the initials of your client and then include the date (i.e., AleHe 2015-08-01). Those suggestions will sort your notebooks chronologically and alphabetically, respectively. All notes contained within a client notebook (with a few exceptions noted later) should use a naming convention starting with the date (i.e., 2015-08-01 Fee Agreement), which is a best practice for any paperless system so that files are sorted in chronological order.

FIGURE 5.13
Pending, Open, Closed, and Non-Engaged Stacks with Client Identifiers

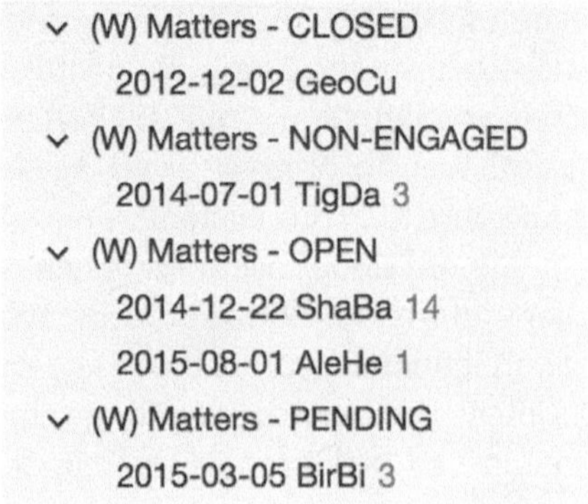

- ⌄ (W) Matters - CLOSED
  - 2012-12-02 GeoCu
- ⌄ (W) Matters - NON-ENGAGED
  - 2014-07-01 TigDa 3
- ⌄ (W) Matters - OPEN
  - 2014-12-22 ShaBa 14
  - 2015-08-01 AleHe 1
- ⌄ (W) Matters - PENDING
  - 2015-03-05 BirBi 3

Pending Matters Stack

The pending matters stack contains notebooks for all potential clients. Notes might contain the following, as shown in Figure 5.14:

- Intake Sheet. The contents of an intake sheet would include client contact information, opposing parties and counsel, related parties and counsel, nature of the matter, and referral information.
- Conflict Check. Use Evernote's search feature to conduct a global conflict check. Assuming you have stored the necessary information on each of your clients in Evernote, any conflict should appear in your search results. Create a note documenting your conflict check—when it was conducted, the results, and discussion of any conflicts necessitating a waiver. If you have multiple lawyers in your firm, they will all need to use Evernote for this system to function properly.
- Non-Engagement Letter or Fee Agreement. Draft a non-engagement letter for a prospective client you decide not to represent, or draft a fee agreement for a client you plan to represent. Once you finalize this document and receive signatures, save the final version as a PDF.

FIGURE 5.14

Sample Pending Matter Notebook with Notes

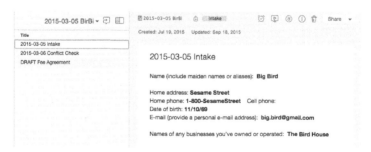

If a potential client becomes a client, then you would move that notebook to your open matters stack. If you decide not to represent the client, then you can place the notebook in your stack for non-engaged matters. If the potential client returns to you at a later date, you'll have information to reference; if they've given you confidential information, you'll want to be certain that it doesn't later conflict you out of another matter (i.e., spouse in divorce matter); and of course if there's ever an ethics or malpractice claim against you, you'll want this information for the record.

Open Matters Stack—Client Notebooks

Here's what you might find in one of your client notebooks:

- Intake, Conflict Check, and Fee Agreement. All these documents will have been moved from your Pending Matters stack. If you use Evernote to store drafts, revisions, final executed copies of your fee agreements, and addenda, this would be a good opportunity to use a tag labeled `fee agreement`. That way, if you need to find all fee agreements documents associated with this matter, a simple search for the `fee agreement` tag within that notebook would result in all the relevant documents.
- Case Timeline. Throughout the life cycle of a matter, you'll update your case timeline many times. Evernote is an ideal place to draft and revise your case timeline when necessary. Since there is no corresponding date associated with the case timeline, entitle it Case Timeline. From the note attributes, you can determine when the case timeline was last updated.
- Statute of Limitations. Here's where Evernote's reminder function comes in handy. Use a note to identify the statute of limitations for the matter. Set a check-in reminder for some time before the statute has run (six weeks or so).
- Attorney Notes. Label your attorney notes starting with the date for sorting and searching purposes. Add the tag `attorney notes` for further organization.
- Work Product. You might store both drafts and final work product documents in an open matters notebook. Use tags for the different types of document, such as `deposition`

`materials`, `motion`, `brief`, and so on. For drafts, clearly identify the document as a draft in the title. Finalized documents should always include the date. One good use of internal note links (as discussed in Section 2.4) is with, for example, a deposition outline. When drafting your outline, include live references to other important documents in Evernote via note links (i.e., depositions on file, exhibits).

- Correspondence. Draft correspondence and save PDFs of letters in your client notebook. You can also forward client-related e-mails to your client notebook for reference.
- Client Documents. Scan in and save your client documents as PDFs. Use consistent naming conventions and tags to identify the type of document.
- Annotated Documents. Say you receive a purchase and sale agreement that you need to mark up. Save it to Evernote, use Evernote's annotation tool (Premium only) to mark up the document, and then share it with a colleague or opposing counsel.

Figure 5.15 provides a sample open matter client notebook with notes as described above.

FIGURE 5.15
Sample Open Matter Client Notebook with Notes

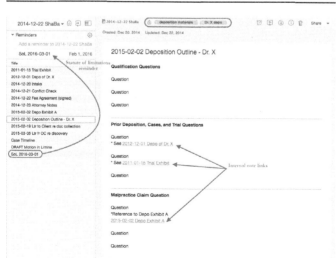

Closed Matters Stack

Once you've closed a matter, you'll want to retain the contents of that file, at least for a period of time. However, if you are using notebooks for each new matter and retain all your closed matter notebooks, you may soon run up against your 250-notebook limit. One way to avoid this is to move your closed matters to a stack labeled Closed Matters for temporary holding. Then, institute a workflow for exporting the contents of the closed matter notebook and archiving it outside of Evernote to a server, hard drive, or cloud storage. This method is analogous to closing a paper file and sending it to be stored offsite, except that it doesn't cost nearly as much to archive your Evernote notes and you can access them anytime with ease. For more on exporting data, see Section 6.4.

5.3 Legal Research

Evernote's Web Clipper, tagging, and search features make it an excellent tool for storing and organizing legal research. This is possibly the most common use of Evernote by lawyers. Rather than searching one by one through that stack of printed case law each time you need to reference your research, you can use Evernote as a central repository. Use Evernote's Web Clipper and e-mail to Evernote to send research such as case law, statutes, and articles to Evernote. Remember to name your legal research notes in a consistent fashion (typically by citation). There are many ways to organize your legal research in Evernote. Here are two simple ways:

1. Store relevant research within individual client matter notebooks (as described in the previous section). Tag all research notes according to their subject matter. When you need it, a search within that notebook for a certain tag will result in the relevant research.
2. Store all your research in a notebook or stack labeled "Legal Research." You could (a) place all legal research into one notebook and use tags to identify each note, or (b) create a stack for subject-matter legal research notebooks containing notes further sorted with tags by case proposition, fact pattern, jurisdiction, and client (see Figures 5.16 and 5.17).

FIGURE 5.16
Legal Research Notebook Example

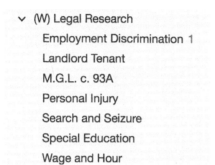

∨ (W) Legal Research
   Employment Discrimination 1
   Landlord Tenant
   M.G.L. c. 93A
   Personal Injury
   Search and Seizure
   Special Education
   Wage and Hour

FIGURE 5.17
Using Tags to Categorize Legal Research

5.4 Marketing

Evernote works well to track your firm's marketing efforts. First, create a notebook stack dedicated to marketing. Within that stack, create notebooks for different areas of your marketing, using titles such as Blog, E-Newsletter, Ideas, Networking, Plans and Reports, and any project-specific marketing (e.g., Writing - Bar Association Newsletter Column), as shown in Figure 5.18. Let's take a look at each of these notebooks.

- Blog. Here's where you keep everything associated with your blog. That might be draft blog posts for collaboration, as well as published posts for archiving. You could also store ideas for your blog, such as relevant articles/blog posts, research, and a checklist of blog ideas (see Figure 5.19).
- E-Newsletter. Keep your research for future newsletters, draft content, contact lists, and sent newsletters as an archive.
- Ideas. Store marketing ideas in this notebook. Notes might include a photo of an effective print advertisement, web clip of a popular lawyer website or blog, running list of ideas for presentations, and articles about how to market a law practice.

FIGURE 5.18
Marketing Notebook Example

FIGURE 5.19
Blog Notebook and Blog Post Idea
Checklist Note

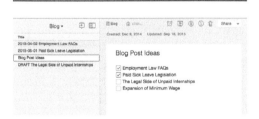

- Networking. Save notes for networking purposes, including a list of networking events that you'd like to attend, lists of your top referral sources, articles that you plan to send to contacts, notes for networking events (i.e., research on speakers and attendees), and business cards with notes.
- Plans and Reports. Your firm's marketing plan can go here, enabling you to share and collaborate with others, as well as revise it as needed. Download return on investment reports from your marketing sources, such as Google Analytics, Facebook, and Twitter.
- Project-Specific Notebooks. For substantive projects, such as writing a monthly column in your bar association's newsletter or giving a presentation at a conference, create a separate notebook for that specific project. Store all your research, materials, e-mails, and drafts there, as shown in Figure 5.20.

FIGURE 5.20
Project-Specific Notebook with Notes

5.5 Productivity and Time Management

By providing a central repository for data, remote access, and quick capture, Evernote acts as a productivity tool for lawyers. This section provides a few specific ways in which Evernote can help lawyers better manage their time.

Read Later

How many times have you come across an e-mail or web article that you'd like to read, but haven't had the time? It's impossible to stay on top of all the reading you need to do. With Evernote, you can quickly capture reading for later with the Web Clipper, e-mail, or print to Evernote/import folders and categorize your reading with tags. Either you can create a dedicated notebook to store your items for reading later (Read Later), or you can save reading in multiple folders and use a read later tag for search purposes. No matter which way you choose, when you have some time, whether you are at your office or on the go, all of your reading will be waiting for you in Evernote.

Checklists

Evernote's checkbox formatting feature is perfect for creating checklists. You can use checklists in your practice for tasks, procedures, marketing, and processes specific to your practice area. For example, create a Blog Post checklist that contains the steps you need to take when you post to your blog—draft post, add images, finalize post, post to blog, post to social media, and include in a newsletter. Use this checklist as a template and then copy it to the appropriate notebook (i.e., Blog) each time you need to use it. Now, rather than remembering to do each of these items, you can check them off one by one when you've accomplished them or collaborate with staff members so that you know when each one has been completed.

Checklists work well for administrative procedures such as conflict checking and practice-area processes such as filing a trademark or drafting and filing a 12(b)(6) motion. Of course, you can also use checklists for your to-do items. Each client notebook could have its own to-do list. Keep your to-do list at the very top of the note list by titling it !To-Do. As long as you sort your notes alphabetically, the punctuation will ensure that your to-do list is consistently filed at the top of the list. Figure 5.21 shows a sample checklist notebook with notes.

FIGURE 5.21
Checklist Notebook Sample with Notes

Getting Things Done

If you are a fan of David Allen's popular task management method, Getting Things Done (GTD), Evernote provides an excellent way to implement it. If you are unfamiliar with the methodology, it is a highly effective time and information management technique for lawyers. The method works in five simple steps, which Allen describes as "apply[ing] order to chaos": Capture, Clarify, Organize, Engage, and Reflect.

The Capture phase begins with a collection of all items you need to get done. You must then Clarify or process what action should be applied to the item. For example, it could be trashed, filed for later, delegated, or, if it takes less than two minutes, completed immediately. The third step, Organize, is when you take that action you defined and move it to the proper category (called a "context") so that you know precisely what it needs when you return to it. For example, if it is an action that requires a phone call, then move it to the category Calls. Now it's time to do some of those actions, or Engage. Finally, you must Reflect upon your lists by reviewing them on a regular basis. For a complete overview, take a look at Allen's website: www.gettingthingsdone.com. As with everything else in Evernote, there is no proper way to set it up for GTD. A number of authors, including Allen, have produced guides for using GTD with Evernote, each with a different suggested setup. Based on research and my own use of Evernote with GTD, I propose the following. While this setup (or any other, for that matter) may not be perfect for you, it will give you some ideas for tailoring Evernote to your own GTD system. Here's the setup based on Allen's five core concepts.

Capture

Begin by collecting items in your default notebook (!Inbox). This should require very little thought, and as discussed previously, information can be dumped easily into Evernote via e-mail, Web Clipper, or by creating a new note from your desktop, mobile device, or wearable.

Clarify

Make it a habit each morning to process your tasks in your default notebook. To remind yourself, add your default notebook (!Inbox) to your shortcuts. Delegate any items as necessary, complete any tasks that take less than two minutes, and convert those remaining into actionable items.

Here's one example of how to process tasks into actionable items. Say you've forwarded an e-mail regarding a bar association article you've agreed to write; then, break that up into actionable items—research, outline, draft, and finalize.

Organize

After processing and defining the actionable tasks, you need to sort them. I suggest using both notebooks and tags for this purpose. Tags work well for today, next, someday/maybe, waiting for actions, and context-specific actions such as anywhere, calls, work, home. Thus, you can assign multiple tags such as today, as well as anywhere. Tasks should also be moved from your default notebook to another notebook, which might be a work notebook, personal notebook, or project-specific notebook.

For example, say you'd like to organize the aforementioned tasks for the bar association article (research, outline, draft, and finalize). Move the tasks to your project-specific notebook Writing - Bar Association, and give the tasks tags such as today, next, and work. If you'd like the tasks sorted in a particular order, then use numeric prefixes to do so (i.e., 01 for research, 02 for outline, 03 for draft). Now you'll have all your tasks associated with the writing assignment in a notebook for reference, but you have also assigned the tasks to tags so that you know when and where you need to get each one done.

Engage

Engaging or doing primarily relies on your tag lists. I would recommend pinning, at least, your today tag to your shortcuts. You'll work from your today shortcut on a daily basis. It's essentially your daily to-do list. With Evernote search, you could also further refine your today list by searching for context tags (or even creating a saved search with, for example, today and work tags for things you need to get done at work today). Evernote reminders are also helpful for keeping track of items with a due date in the future. Rather than dump all your tasks into the next tag, place them into project-specific notebooks and assign reminders so that you'll know when you need to move them to your today or next list (depending on the task's urgency). For example, if that bar association article is due six months from now, set up a reminder for when you'd like to start working on the note (maybe in four months). Once that reminder appears, it's time to tack on a today or next tag. Reminders also work well for recurring items that you don't want sitting on your next tag list in perpetuity, and for waiting for items so that you don't lose track of them.

When you finish with a task, there are a few steps you can take: (1) if you don't need it any longer, delete it completely (it will still reside in your Trash until you empty it); (2) if you don't need it associated with a certain project, but may need it for future reference, place it in an Archive notebook; or (3) if you still want it available, just remove the tag today and it will continue to reside in whatever notebook you've assigned it to, but it will no longer be on your to-do list. View Figure 5.22 for a sample setup of GTD in Evernote.

Using the earlier example of a bar association article, when you have finalized your article, give it a name that's consistent with your naming conventions (i.e., 2015-11-01 E-Discovery in Employment Litigation), add tags (i.e. bar association, publication), and move it to your Archive notebook (see Figure 5.23). You can also do the same with your research and outline, if you wish to save those materials for reference.

FIGURE 5.22
Example Setup of GTD in Evernote

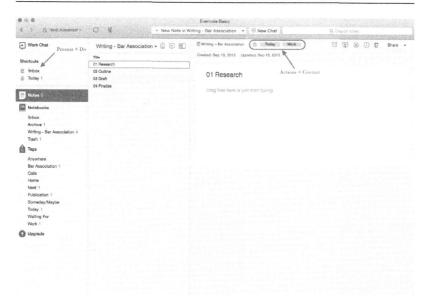

FIGURE 5.23
Archive Notes

Reflect

As with any GTD system, a review is essential. I recommend conducting a weekly review of today, next, someday/maybe, and waiting for tags. Upon your review, you might decide to reassign a tag or delete a task altogether. I would also recommend conducting a review of your project-specific notebooks, on a regular basis, to be sure your tasks are organized appropriately. Conducting a review can be time-consuming and also easily forgotten (or ignored). To ensure that you do it, create a note entitled "GTD Review" and then add a recurring task. Remember that Evernote doesn't have a recurring task feature, so after you've completed your review, set another reminder for the same date/time the following week. This system works well because until you complete your review and set a new reminder for that note, the current reminder will appear at the top of your reminder list.

6

Evernote Security

Is Evernote secure? If you were hoping I'd give you a one-word answer, well, you've come to the wrong place. Just like in law, data security rarely falls into categories of black or white. Rather, it's a question of risk and how much you're willing to accept. No physical or electronic system is 100 percent secure. When you make decisions about security (whether physical or electronic) for your business, you base those decisions on your ethical and statutory obligations, sensitivity of the data, risk tolerance, knowledge and sophistication, safeguards enacted (or to be enacted), and resources, among other factors. Here's where I put on my law practice advisor hat. No one can tell you whether or how you should use a certain cloud service. You must do your own due diligence, and then conduct your own risk analysis to make your determination. My hope is that the discussion in this chapter will help guide you toward a reasoned and intelligent decision.

6.1 Ethical and Statutory Obligations

The consideration of whether and how to use Evernote in your law practice begins with an understanding of your professional and statutory obligations. First, read your state's ethics opinion(s) on the use of the cloud. Most states have explicitly authorized its use, with the requirement or recommendation that lawyers exercise "reasonable care" when storing client data with a cloud provider. For a listing of opinions, see the American Bar Association's Law Technology Resource Center chart of cloud ethics opinions, available at www.americanbar.org/groups/departments_offices/legal_technology _resources/resources/charts_fyis/cloud-ethics-chart.html. Most opinions define the reasonable care standard with a set of factors to apply when deciding whether and how to use a certain provider. Also helpful when conducting your due diligence is the Legal Cloud Computing Association (LCCA) Standards for cloud technology, available at www.legalcloudcomputingassociation.org/standards.

You'll also need to know what statutory duties are required of your business. For example, a number of states aim to protect the personal information of their residents through laws that regulate how businesses use and keep their customer's information. In Massachusetts, one of the strictest data privacy regimes, businesses of any size are required to encrypt certain personal data that is "transmitted wirelessly."[1] This information is highly relevant when deciding whether a certain cloud provider is appropriate for your practice.

6.2 Vetting Evernote

Once you've completed your research and understand your obligations, it's time to take a look at Evernote and see whether it can live up to your respective duties. Evernote should be vetted just like any other cloud provider. First, review Evernote's current policies. Those policies should provide, at least, information about their servers; data backup; security features; data ownership; and third-party access to data. Second, you need to do your own due diligence to investigate the company's reputation, any history of breaches, and any service interruptions. Typically, that information can be found online.

A number of policies are available on the Evernote legal page at www.evernote.com/legal. A good place to start is "Evernote's 3 Laws of Data Protection," which concisely summarizes the company's philosophy regarding the handling of your data. "Evernote's 3 Laws of Data Protection" references the "Terms of Service," "Privacy Policy," and "Transparency Report," which are key documents worth reviewing as part of your vetting process. You might be a lawyer, but most

---

1. 201 C.M.R. 17.00, *see* M.G.L.c. 93H.

lawyers I know despise reading these types of service contracts. Fortunately, Evernote's policies are written in plain language to accommodate all users (maybe a good model for other service contracts; hint hint, lawyer drafters). An entire section of the Evernote website is dedicated to security, available at www.evernote.com/security.

Here are some of the highlights I glean from the policies (reviewed at the date this book was written):

- Data Ownership
  - Evernote does not own your data.
  - By using the program, you grant Evernote a limited license to "displace, perform and distribute your Content and to modify . . . and reproduce such Content to enable Evernote to operate the Service."[2]
  - When your Evernote data is sent to a third party for normal operational purposes, Evernote assures that the third party also protects your ownership rights.

- Data Protection
  - Evernote stores your data in "multiple redundant servers, storage devices and off-site backups" in the United States,[3] which are accessible only to Evernote employees and are audited and monitored around the clock.
  - Data is always encrypted in transit, but not at rest.

- Data Usage
  - Evernote does not give or sell your information for advertising purposes. It monitors your data to provide search functionality, return related notes, and make product recommendations.
  - In response to third-party requests for data, the company will share information. However, according to the "Transparency Report," only a small number of requests for information from a variety of sources are received in a given year; and when the request is made, the company

2. Evernote.com, *Evernote Terms of Service*, www.evernote.com/legal/tos.php.
3. Evernote.com, *Evernote's 3 Laws of Data Protection*, www.evernote.com/legal/data-protection.php.

is committed to "respond[ing] as narrowly as possible under the law."[4] The company also requires a search warrant before disclosing contents of an account and, in most circumstances, will notify a user when Evernote has received a legal request for information.

Evernote has received criticism for not encrypting data at rest—that is, while it's stored on Evernote's servers. Encryption of data at rest is a recognized method of preventing unauthorized access. Although it has chosen not to encrypt at rest, Evernote does have a dedicated security team responsible for maintaining data security. Only Evernote employees have access to their centers, which are monitored 24/7. Evernote has mitigated some risk of potential unauthorized access by controlling its own infrastructure within secure data centers. For more details about the company's security program, see the Security Overview, available at www.evernote.com/security.

Part of the vetting process, and particularly important for those wary of Evernote's unencrypted data at rest policy, is to review the company's incident history to determine just how well the company's security program has fared. In February 2013, the company discovered "suspicious activity on the Evernote network."[5] Hackers had gained access to user names, e-mail addresses, and encrypted passwords, but there was no evidence that any user content had been accessed. As a result, Evernote took action. First, the company initiated a password reset for all users, informing users by e-mail and a published blog post on its website. Second, the company took proactive steps to increase security by implementing two-step authentication (discussed further in Section 6.3). In June 2014, Evernote suffered a "denial of service" attack, where hackers demanded ransom from Evernote in order to maintain operations, which temporarily prevented users from accessing their accounts.[6] There were no reports of unauthorized access to user data or loss of data as a result of this attack.

---

4. Evernote.com, *Evernote's Transparency Policy*, www.evernote.com/legal /transparency.
5. Evernote Blog, *Security Notice: Service-wide Password Reset*, https://blog.evernote .com/blog/2013/03/02/security-notice-service-wide-password-reset.
6. Forbes, *Evernote Pounded by Aggressive Cyber Attack*, http://www.forbes.com /sites/leoking/2014/06/11/evernote-pounded-by-aggressive-cyber-attack.

For each incident, Evernote responded promptly and made users aware of the problems. After an in-depth look at Evernote's policies, procedures, and incident history, my takeaway is that Evernote demonstrates a commitment to security, provides transparent and understandable terms of usage, and notifies the community when problems arise. Notwithstanding Evernote's commitment to security, there are ways in which Evernote users can enhance the security of their individual accounts and thus further minimize risk of unauthorized access to data.

6.3 Securing Evernote

To reduce the risk of unauthorized access to your Evernote data, there are a number of steps that you should consider implementing, particularly if you store client data in Evernote.

Create Strong Passwords

A strong password is the number one best line of defense against unauthorized access to your data in Evernote (and, any other online service, for that matter). Elements of a strong password include the following:

- It is unique; used for this service only.
- It is long and uses a variety of characters.
- Is not a common word or phrase.

The best type of password is one that is randomly generated. You can do this with many password managers such as 1Password, LastPass, Dashlane, KeyPass, and iCloud Keychain.

Use Two-Step Verification

Two-step verification is available for all Evernote users. It works like an ATM card used to retrieve cash from an ATM—first, you must swipe your card, then you must enter your personal identification number (PIN). Two-step verification requires something you know (i.e., PIN or password), in addition to something you have in your physical possession (i.e., your ATM card or mobile device), thus creating a stronger security barrier. Set up two-step verification by logging into your Evernote web account and selecting Security Summary from your Account Settings. Then enable two-step verification (see Figure 6.1). Evernote will provide you with a list of backup codes, should you ever need to log into your account and do not have your mobile device available. To log in with two-step verification, you'll enter your user name and password and then either use a verification code generation app, such as Google Authenticator (see Figure 6.2), or opt to receive a text message with your code (only for Plus and Premium users). Once you complete the two-step verification for that device, Evernote will authorize that device and remember it for future logins (thus only requiring your user name and password).

FIGURE 6.1
Set Up Two-Step Verification (Web)

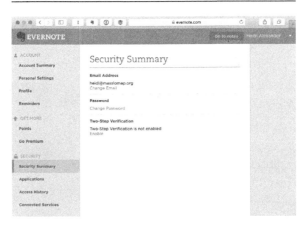

FIGURE 6.2
Use Two-Step Verification (Web)

Set a Passcode Lock

This feature is available for mobile devices only. Once it's activated from the Preferences/Settings pane of your device, each time you open Evernote on your mobile device, you will be prompted to enter a four-digit code or to unlock with your iOS Touch ID. This provides an extra protection in case of a lost or stolen device.

Use Text Encryption

Evernote offers a feature to encrypt text within a note. Highlight the text you'd like to encrypt, right-click, and select Encrypt Selected Text (see Figure 6.3); or, highlight the text and then navigate from

FIGURE 6.3
Highlight Text for Encryption

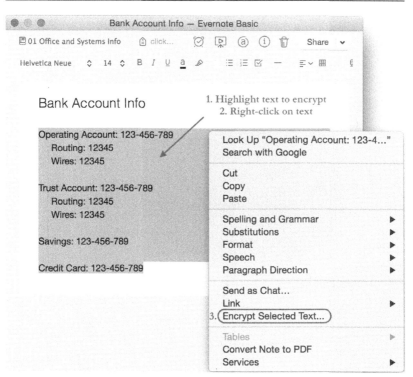

your application menu to Edit (Mac) or Format (Windows) and then select Encrypt Selected Text. See Figure 6.4 (Mac) and Figure 6.5 (Windows).

You can also use the shortcut to encrypt text: ⇧⌘X (Mac) or Ctrl + Shift + X (Windows). Then, set the passphrase for decrypting your text and a hint, if so desired (see Figure 6.6). Evernote does not store your passphrase. This prevents even the company from accessing encrypted content. However, if you lose your passphrase you are out

FIGURE 6.4
Encrypt Text from Application Menu (Mac)

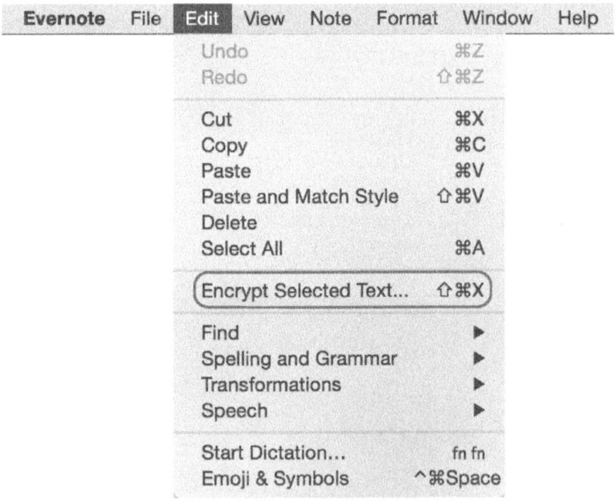

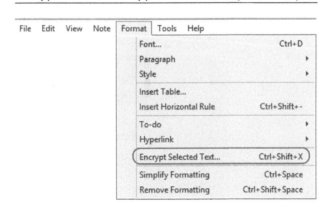

FIGURE 6.5
Encrypt Text from Application Menu (Windows)

of luck, so you should save your passphrase(s) in a password manager. If you select "Remember passphrase until I quit Evernote," you won't need to enter the passphrase until the next time you close out and reopen the application.

You can view the encrypted text from any device by clicking on the encrypted selection (see Figure 6.7) and then selecting "Show encrypted text" (see Figure 6.8).

FIGURE 6.6
Set Passphrase and Hint

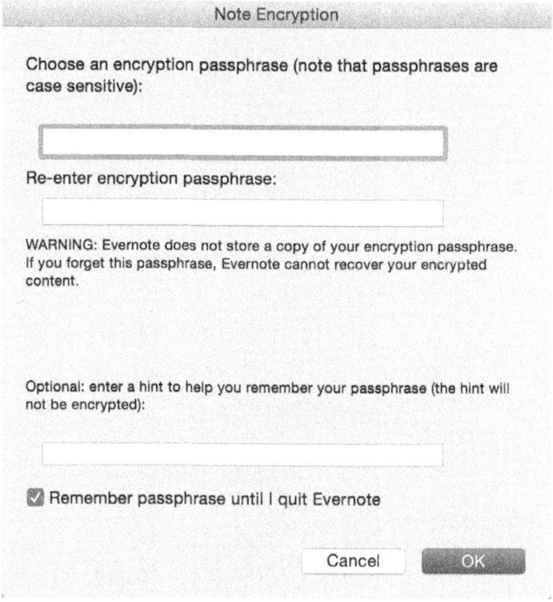

Note Encryption

Choose an encryption passphrase (note that passphrases are case sensitive):

Re-enter encryption passphrase:

WARNING: Evernote does not store a copy of your encryption passphrase. If you forget this passphrase, Evernote cannot recover your encrypted content.

Optional: enter a hint to help you remember your passphrase (the hint will not be encrypted):

☑ Remember passphrase until I quit Evernote

Cancel   OK

FIGURE 6.7
Encrypted Text

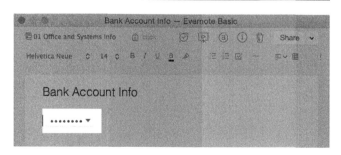

Bank Account Info — Evernote Basic

01 Office and Systems Info   click   Share ⌄

Helvetica Neue   14   B I U a

Bank Account Info

•••••••• ▼

FIGURE 6.8
Show Encrypted Text

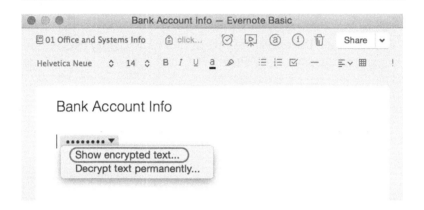

Next, you'll be prompted for the passphrase (see Figure 6.9). Enter the passphrase, and the text will appear. You can turn off encryption anytime you decide you no longer wish to encrypt that text; choose "Decrypt text permanently" from the drop-down menu when clicking on the text.

FIGURE 6.9
Enter Passphrase to Show Encrypted Text

Other Security Options

- *Use Local Notebooks.* To prevent Evernote from storing your data on its server, you can opt to create only local notebooks that will store your data solely on your hard drive. However, because local notebooks do not sync, they are accessible only from your computer and not from any other device. To further protect those local notebooks, you could then choose to encrypt your local Evernote database or even your entire hard drive. You'll also want to be sure to back up your local database (see Section 6.4).

- *Monitor Access History.* From your Account Settings via Evernote web, you can view which Evernote platform was accessed, when, and from what IP address and location. Any suspicious unauthorized activity could be discovered here.
- *Manage Authorized Applications.* Also from your Account Settings via Evernote web, you can view all applications (i.e., devices and browsers) that have access to your account. From there, you can revoke access to applications if you lose a device or see a suspicious device on the list that is not your own.

6.4 Backing Up Evernote Data

Backing up your Evernote data should be part of your security regimen. Even though your data syncs with Evernote's servers, if there should ever be a problem with its servers or with your data, you could lose everything. Having a backup of your Evernote data will avoid frustration down the road. Plus, it's easy to accomplish. There are two ways to back up your Evernote data: you can back up your hard drive or export your notes from Evernote.

Backing Up Your Hard Drive

If you regularly back up your entire computer hard drive, that should include a backup of your Evernote data directory. If you ever need to restore your data, you'll need to know the location of your Evernote data directory. By restoring your entire Evernote database, you'll preserve your notebook structure and tags. You can typically find your Evernote data library in one of the places indicated in the following directories for Mac and Windows.

Windows

C:\ Users \ [PC Name] \ AppData \ Local \ Evernote \ Databases

Mac

/ Users / [Your Username] / Library / Application Support / Evernote

/ Users / [Your Username] / Library / Containers / com.evernote. Evernote

/ Users / [Your Username] / Library / Application Support / com. evernote.Evernote

In recent versions of Mac OS, Apple hides the Library folder. To view the Library folder and other hidden files, you can either use a Terminal command or change a setting in the Finder window.

- Using Terminal command (see Figure 6.10):
  - In Applications > Utilities > Terminal, type the following command and enter/return:

  defaults write com.apple.finder AppleShowAllFiles YES

  - To hide files again, type the following command in Terminal and enter/return:

  defaults write com.apple.finder AppleShowAllFiles NO

FIGURE 6.10
Terminal Command—Show Library Folder

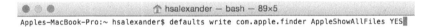

```
● ● ●                    ⬆ hsalexander — bash — 89×5
Apples-MacBook-Pro:~ hsalexander$ defaults write com.apple.finder AppleShowAllFiles YES█
```

- Using Finder (see Figure 6.11):
  1. Open a new Finder window.
  2. From the Finder menu, select Go > Home.
  3. From the Finder menu, select View > Show View Options.
  4. Check the box for Show Library Folder.

FIGURE 6.11
Show Library Folder from Finder

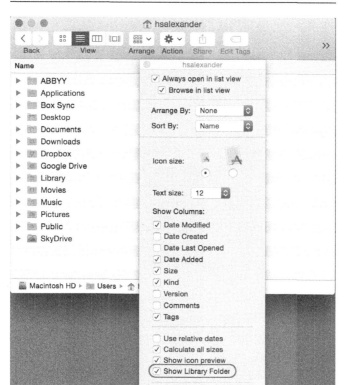

Export Notes from Evernote

You can export all your notes, individual notes, or selected notebooks from within Evernote in XML or HTML format. Exporting your notes from Evernote has some unique advantages and disadvantages.

Exporting All Notes, Selected Notebooks, and Individual Notes

- Exporting all notes is the simplest and quickest way to back up your notes. The downside is that you'll lose the notebook structure if/when restoring these notes.
- Exporting selected notebooks is more tedious than exporting all notes at once. But, the advantage is that you can preserve your notebook structure and restore individual notebooks.

- Exporting individual notes is also tedious, but it will enable you to restore individual notes, if need be.

Exporting to XML or HTML Format

- Exporting to Evernote XML format is best for backup purposes because it preserves all note formatting in one XML file for re-importing into Evernote. This format works well for backup, migrating data to another Evernote account, or archiving data.
- Exporting to HTML allows you to capture your notes in a format that is not specific to Evernote and thus could be accessed without Evernote. The disadvantage is that HTML does not preserve the original note formatting, tag, or notebook structure. Export to HTML will produce multiple files based on the contents of the note. For example, note attachments and images will appear in a separate .resources folder. If you export multiple notes or notebooks to HTML, an .index.html file will also be created to display a listing of, with links to, all notes exported in that batch. Figure 6.12 shows a sample client notebook exported in HTML format.

FIGURE 6.12
Export to HTML Format

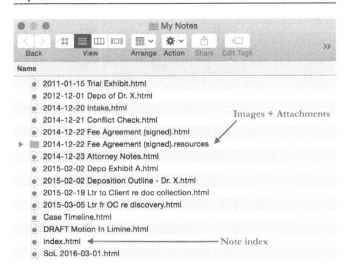

Export Instructions for Mac Users

To export all notes, follow these steps (see Figure 6.13):

1. From the Evernote application menu, select View > Show All Notes (or, use the shortcut ⇧⌘A).
2. Select Edit > Select All (or, use the shortcut ⌘A).
3. Go to File > Export Notes (or, right-click on Notes and select Export Notes).
4. You'll then be prompted to save your notes in a certain format: Evernote XML or HTML. If saving to the XML format, you can check the box under Format to preserve your tags.

To export individual notebooks: from the notebooks view, right-click on the notebook you'd like to export and select Export Notes. Then, follow the instructions above, beginning at step 4.

To export individual notes: from your note list, right-click on the note that you wish to export and select Export Note. Then, follow step 4 of the instructions above.

FIGURE 6.13
Export All Notes

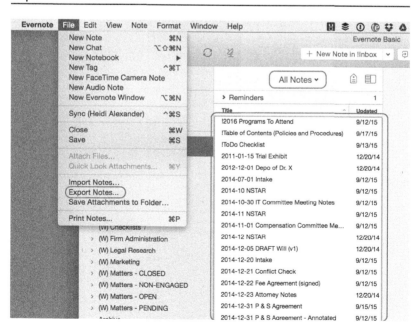

Export Instructions for Windows Users

To export all notes, follow these steps (see Figures 6.14 and 6.15):

1. From the Evernote application menu, select View > Notes (or use the shortcut Ctrl + Shift + Alt + N). Then, select Edit > Select All (or use the shortcut Ctrl + A).
2. Go to File > Export (or right-click on Notes and then select Export Notes).
3. You'll then be prompted to save your notes as an Evernote XML or HTML, along with a couple of additional optional formats (described in the prompt box). Click on Options to check which formatting features you'd like to preserve (different options accompany different formatting options— i.e., title, created date, updated date, location, author, location, tags, source URL).

To export individual notebooks: from the sidebar or notebooks view, right-click on the notebook you'd like to export and select Export Notes. Then, follow the instructions above in step 3.

To export individual notes: from your note list, right-click on the note you wish to export and select Export Note. Then, follow the instructions above in step 3.

FIGURE 6.14

File > Export (Windows)

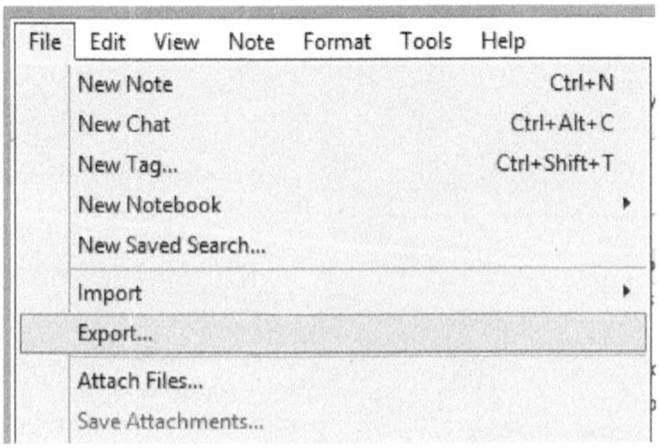

FIGURE 6.15
Export Options (Windows)

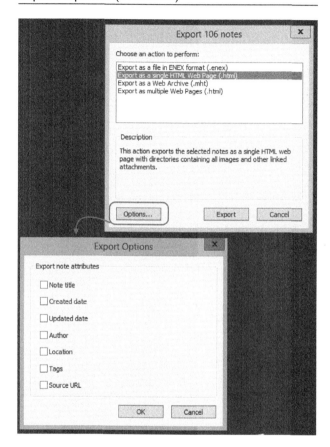

Beyond the Lessons: Real-Life Examples of Evernote in Law Practice

Throughout this book, I've outlined a number of ways that you can use Evernote in your law practice, focusing on the most popular types of uses for lawyers. But, I don't purport to have covered every possible method. Every lawyer must tailor Evernote to his or her own practice. To demonstrate that, I enlisted assistance from a few lawyers who use Evernote daily in their law practices. In this chapter, these lawyers describe how they use Evernote in their practices and share their best practice tips based on their own experiences with Evernote. Hopefully, these lawyers will provide you with additional ideas on how to incorporate Evernote into your workflow.

7.1 Joseph Bahgat

Joseph Bahgat is a lawyer at HubCity Law Group with offices in New Jersey and Ohio. He provides organizations and creative professionals with legal advice in the areas of business consultation and litigation, Internet-related controversies, and contracts and licensing agreements. Joe publishes the blog "Internet on Trial" (www.internetontrial.com).

How Joe Uses Evernote in His Law Practice

Daily Notebook

Every day when I get to my computer (or sometimes not until the phone rings for the first time!), I create a new note in my .daily notebook, which is blank, but titled with the day's date. I've been meaning to automate this task, but haven't gotten around to it yet. For now, I just open Evernote and click the + New Note in .daily button; then I have a keyboard shortcut to enter today's date as 2015-09-01. When the phone rings, I have another keyboard shortcut to enter the current time, and then I just type notes from the call. I have my own shorthand, but it's not too crazy. If the caller is a potential client I try to gather as much info as possible about them, and if I make any suggestions, or quote a fee, I make sure to put that in my notes also. If the caller is court/judicial staff, opposing counsel, etc., the notes are usually task related, so I'll add a reminder. At the end of the day (or week sometimes), I go back and review the daily phone logs to see whether anything has slipped through the cracks. Usually I'll send the task-related data to OmniFocus (for Mac and iOS), but sometimes I'll keep it in Evernote. I'm more likely to leave it in Evernote if there's a document attached to it, because, for whatever reason, I feel like it's easier to deal with attachments in Evernote than it is in OmniFocus.

Drafts Notebook

Anytime I have an idea for something I need to write, whether it's an appellate brief, letter to opposing counsel, blog post, or even an e-mail I want to send someone, that idea usually starts out in Evernote, in my .drafts notebook. It's especially great for blogging because I don't have to worry about WordPress crashing, or losing my Internet connection, etc. (I've lost way too many great blog posts to similar occurrences!). Evernote is also useful for blogging because it can store any image files or PDFs I want to link to in the post.

Case Law and Statutory Repository

Every case, statute, or treatise excerpt I e-mail to myself from Westlaw automatically goes into Evernote. It took me a while to get in this habit, but once I did it has really paid off. The benefit isn't just having everything in the same place, either. The reason I love Evernote to keep all this stuff is because of the tags! It's too hard to put all the relevant info about a case into the file name, especially when the case is useful for several different propositions of law. Using Evernote, I created tags for legal subtopics and issues, which makes it really easy to find my past research when I need to. Ideally, I apply a set of tags to every opinion: (1) jurisdiction tags, identifying the state name if it's a state law issue that's relevant, whether it's state or federal court, etc.; (2) judge name(s) (if relevant); (3) whether there's a circuit split, or if it's a majority/minority opinion; (4) the legal topics/subtopics covered, e.g., personal jurisdiction, serving subpoena or process on a website operator, expectation of privacy, First Amendment, etc.; (5) procedural issue, e.g., the type of motion being examined, weight of the evidence; and (6) any other relevant information or buzzwords that I want to quickly search for in the future.

Joe's Best Practice Tips

I find that Evernote is great for keeping many kinds of checklists, for example, when I'm building a trial notebook, or preparing for a deposition or settlement conference. In addition to the fact that Evernote lets me easily reuse templates from other cases or projects, the thing I really like about Evernote for these checklists is that I can still see the items that have been checked off.

7.2 Ben Carter

Ben Carter runs his own law firm, Ben Carter Law PLLC (www .bencarterlaw.com), in Louisville, Kentucky. He practices in the areas of foreclosure defense, consumer law, bankruptcy, election law, and personal injury. He also co-hosts a podcast called "Let's Start a Law Firm."

How Ben Uses Evernote in His Law Practice

The problem with saving legal research is that it's difficult to create a useful taxonomy for the stuff. When saving cases, should I save it in a subfolder in the case I'm working on? That seems logical but then retrieving the case years later will require me to remember exactly what case I was working on when I came across "that one case that stood for [insert legal issue] proposition."

If instead (or additionally), I opt to save it under the legal issue the case stands for, what should I do when the case stands for two important propositions? Kentucky attorneys will obviously know that *Steelvest, Inc. v. Scansteel Service Center, Inc.* gives us our summary judgment standard in state court. But, it also states that a breach of fiduciary duty is tantamount to fraud. As a consumer advocate, this is an important part of the case. Do I save *Steelvest* in three places: the client file, the research file on summary judgment, and the research file on breach of fiduciary duty?

No.

I save it to Evernote by e-mailing it from my online research service using a special e-mail address Evernote provides. When I e-mail that case to Evernote, the .pdf is automatically processed in OCR so that a later search for any word in the case will yield results. This means if I can just remember a snippet of language or even what judge decided the case or attorney argued the case, I can search in Evernote and find the case. (I also have a spotless .pdf that I can attach to motions and memoranda.)

Even better, though, than the automatic OCR is Evernote's organizational tools. Evernote gives users the option of placing notes in notebooks (folders) as well as tagging the notes. This means that I can e-mail *Steelvest* to my Evernote account, save it to a client's notebook, and tag it with the tags `summary judgment` and `bofd` (my shorthand for "breach of fiduciary duty"). Later, I can retrieve that case in one of three ways: I can remember the client notebook the case is saved in, I can find the case by reviewing the cases that have a particular tag, or I can search for the case in the search window using words that are likely in the language of the case.

Ben's Best Practice Tips

Evernote gives you the ability to send a case to a notebook with certain tags in the subject line of the e-mail you send to Evernote.

So, in one step, I am able to put the filed, tagged, OCR *Steelvest* case into Evernote by e-mailing it to myself with this subject line: Steelvest @clientname #summary judgment #bofd.

7.3 Jay Fleischman

Jay Fleischman is a partner at Shaev & Fleishman LLP (www .consumerhelpcentral.com), a firm with offices in Los Angeles and New York City. He concentrates his practice on student loan law, consumer bankruptcy, credit reporting, and debt collection harassment. He is the host of the podcast "Consumer Ledger" (www.consumer ledger.com) and co-founder of the Bankruptcy Law Network (www .bankruptcylawnetwork.com). Jay has presented on and written about using Evernote in practice.

How Jay Uses Evernote in His Law Practice

I create a notebook for each of my client matters, then set up a rule in my e-mail program that automatically sends a copy of each client e-mail to that notebook. Sharing the notebook with other people in my firm allows us all to have a fully searchable repository at our disposal.

I am also an avid user of Google Scholar Alerts, which automatically sends me new decisions that match my particular search queries. My Scholar Alerts are set up to send those new decisions to Evernote so I can store and refer to the latest case law whenever I need it.

Finally, the Web Clipper feature of Evernote is something that has become one of my most often used features of any application. I can grab an article, a PDF, a picture, anything at all, and save it directly to Evernote.

Jay's Best Practice Tips

Use the e-mail address that Evernote assigns to you, and set up rules to forward important e-mails to your Evernote account. No matter how good your e-mail search feature gets, it's otherwise difficult to share your messages with others in your office who may need access to the information.

7.4 Katie Floyd

Katie Floyd is a litigation lawyer in Florida, co-host of the Mac Power Users podcast (www.relay.fm/mpu), blogger at www.katiefloyd.com, and consultant on all things Apple and technology related. Katie is a frequent speaker on Evernote and has written numerous articles on the subject.

How Katie Uses Evernote in Her Law Practice

I use Evernote for practice administration tasks. This includes things like keeping track of contracts with vendors, office policies, product manuals, and other general information. I can share this notebook with my law partners and our office administrator to make sure everyone has access.

The attorneys in our office have a weekly breakfast meeting on Wednesday morning to catch up on firm business and review any matters that need attention. This can include a review of cases, discussion of an office expense, or employee reviews. As matters come up throughout the week that would be appropriate for discussion, I send them to Evernote in a notebook called "Wednesday Morning Meetings." If a request comes in via e-mail, I can forward it directly to Evernote; sometimes I'll drag and drop items. Each Wednesday morning I'll carry my iPad to breakfast and scroll through the notebook to have on hand the items we need to review.

I also use Evernote as a repository for information I pick up at CLE courses. Many times I'll attend CLEs and they'll offer downloads of materials. These can included PDFs, PowerPoint documents, and sometimes sample forms. I stick all these documents in Evernote where they can be tagged based on the topic of the course. Evernote does all the heavy lifting by scanning the contents of the documents and making them searchable. Evernote has very powerful search capabilities. So in the future if I need to go back and try to find information I remember was covered in a CLE, all I have to do is search my Evernote database.

Katie's Best Practice Tips

1. In combination with e-mail to Evernote, I use TextExpander to help streamline this process. By modifying the subject of

the e-mail sent to Evernote, you can change the title of the note or file a note in the specific notebook.

The subject of the e-mail will become the title of the note in Evernote. You can also use the @ symbol to designate a specific notebook. For example, adding @ work to the end of the subject line of my e-mail will file that e-mail in my work notebook.

I have specific ways I like to title most of my notes, starting with a numerical date such as 2015.12.15 and then a brief description of the note. I then end with the notebook where the item is going to be filed. To keep consistent, I've created a TextExpander snippet that pre-populates the current date, has a blank fill-in snippet for me to type the subject, and then ends with a drop-down menu to allow me to choose my frequently used notebooks (see Figure 7.1).

FIGURE 7.1

Text Expander Snippet

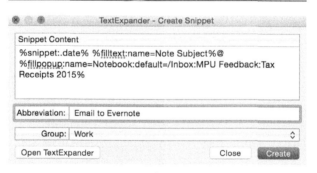

2. Perhaps my favorite and geekiest method for taking advantage of organizing items with Evernote is to use Hazel (for Mac) to automate the process. I described this process in an article I wrote for *Macworld* magazine in 2013 (http://goo.gl/nWBh5F). In short, Hazel monitors a scanned documents folder and when it finds documents that match certain criteria you've previously set up (like a utility, benefits statement, or other document you regularly scan), it will automatically rename, tag, and file these documents

into Evernote. I love this method because it requires no interaction from the user other than initiating the scan. See Figure 7.2 for an example of a Hazel rule for saving documents to Evernote.

FIGURE 7.2
Hazel Rule

7.5 Philippe Doyle Gray

Philippe Doyle Gray is a barrister from Sydney, Australia (www .philippedoylegray.com). His practice focuses on civil litigation in the areas of commercial equity, corporate fraud, and building and construction. Philippe has given multiple presentations and written extensively about Evernote, including for the American Bar Association's TECHSHOW conference.

How Philippe Uses Evernote in His Law Practice

I use Evernote generally for civil litigation in court—to act as a repository for all my professional reading, and to act as a repository for my case headnotes.

Let's first consider professional reading. I use Evernote as a single repository for all my professional reading: seminar papers, presentation slides, blog posts, journal articles, instructional e-mails from colleagues, etc. Sometimes I read and annotate a piece of writing that I file into Evernote, but other times I don't have time to do that so I just file it away into Evernote to be retrieved (and read carefully) when the time comes. And that is the point: when the time comes, I have a (sometimes vague) recollection of having read something about a topic relevant to the matter at hand, but I can find the material when I need to. For example, I might have a seminar paper about the "business records exception" to the rule against hearsay provided by the Evidence Act 1995 (NSW). When I have a trial in which I want to tender business records into evidence, I can quickly find it in Evernote and then read the materials I previously uploaded.

Now let's distinguish headnotes—short summaries, and often selective quotations, of persuasive cases about particular points of law. My case law library is in PDF; I have converted my principal leather-bound volumes of reported cases into an organized collection of PDFs. All other cases that I am using in a matter, if they are not already in any of these law reports, are also converted into PDF and filed away into my law library. If a case is relevant to a matter, then I make an alias (the Mac OS X equivalent of a Windows shortcut) of the PDF file, and file that alias into the folder structure pertaining to the matter. But in the absence of a present matter before the court, there is no folder into which to file an alias of a case that takes my interest. I can file the PDF of the case into my law library, but how do I find it again? I treat the case like a seminar paper—not presently useful, but potentially useful in future. So instead, I make a headnote and place it into Evernote.

The headnote allows me to create something memorable—words that I associate with the ideas in the case. I then add the full citation, and usually a hyperlink. And it is this combination of your own words and the hyperlink that make Evernote useful. Your own words make it easy to retrieve the Evernote from your collection, and the hyperlink makes it easy to retrieve the full text of the law report—either from an on-line database or from my PDF law library. How? Because my PDF law library is stored in Dropbox, and Dropbox allows me to generate a unique URL for a particular file (case) that I then insert into an Evernote. You can see an example of this from my own collection (see Figure 7.3)—this is a case about direct speech in affidavits, *LMI v Baulderstone* [2001] NSWSC 688; 53 NSWLR 31. When you click on *LMI v Baulderstone* [2001] NSWSC 688, you will be taken to the online database report of the case, and if you click on 53 NSWLR 31, you will be taken to the PDF report of the case inside my law library.

FIGURE 7.3
Headnote Case Law Example

Philippe's Best Practice Tips

I recommend creating two new notebooks, one called Inbox and the second called Archive. Make Inbox your default notebook. Any new notes will automatically find their way into the Inbox. When the time comes for you to curate your collection, you can simply click on the Inbox notebook and see every note that requires curation. As you curate the notes, you will assign that note to a different notebook.

If you want to show off, you can change the name of the Inbox notebook to !nbox. If you sort notebooks by name, the ! character will ensure that the notebook appears at the very top, while at the same time it will closely resemble the word *Inbox*. Be warned, if you are sharing that notebook it will not work, and searching by interrogating the index for the word *Inbox* will not result in that notebook being a hit. Perhaps a safer approach is to call that notebook !Inbox.

The Archive notebook is midway between your other notebooks and the trash notebook. It contains notes that you don't want cluttering up your day-to-day use, but that you do want turning up in searches (notes in the Trash notebook do not turn up in searches). In my Evernote collection, I have notes that contain instructions on how to do something, and those instructions include a series of screenshots, as shown in Figures 7.4 and 7.5. The way I create those notes is to create individual screenshots that themselves make up one note. I then compile the instructions by dragging screenshot images from those individual notes. I may want to recycle or edit the image in future, so those screenshot images go into Archive, and the instruction or note goes into an appropriate notebook.

FIGURE 7.4
Instructions Example

Contact details   Report Spam
Updated on 6th 2014

When providing me with contact details, please provide the following information:
1. Honorifics (e.g. The Hon. Justice, Judge, Sir, Dr etc. Do NOT include Mr, Mrs etc. unless the person is concerned with that)
2. First name
3. Last name
4. Post nominals (e.g. QC, SC, MP etc.)
5. Job Title
6. Company
7. Email address (work)
8. Telephone (work) with area code (and country code if not from Australia)
9. Mobile (work) (and country code if not from Australia) - if you can got it - sometimes go to the company website
10. Website - profile page, or if not available, then Website - company (to see the difference between these types, click here and here)
11. Street address - work
12. Photo from website if any
13. Assistant - first and last name
14. Email address (assistant)

SPECIAL RULES FOR LAWYERS AND JUDGES
1. Contact details for lawyers and judges can be found here
2. Job Title for judges, use "Judge" unless they have another title, such as "Chief Justice" or "Chief Judge in Equity" in which case use that title
3. Company for judges, use their Court; for barristers, use their chambers; for solicitors use their firm. Go the official website and check the official name of the court/chambers/firm.
4. Assistant, for judges, use their associate
5. Email address (assistant), for judges, use their associate

For example:

The Hon. Justice Geoff Lindsay
Judge
Supreme Court of New South Wales
JusticeLindsay@courts.nsw.gov.au
ShariWilliams@courts.nsw.gov.au
(02) 9230 8701
http://www.supremecourt.lawlink.nsw.gov.au/supremecourt/sco2_index.html
Law Courts Building 184 Phillip Street Sydney NSW 2000
Shari Williams

Further learning: Farley file

FIGURE 7.5
Instructions Example with Screenshots

How to make a list of authorities - step by step   Report Spam
guide
Updated Apr 26th, 2014

This is a step-by-step guide to combining different PDF files into one single PDF file, arranged in a way that will be useful in Court.

The file created at the end is commonly known as a "binder."

The binder can be used digitally (e.g. on an iPad), but it can also be used *to print* a bundle of authorities to be inserted into a lever-arch folder with a cover sheet, table of contents and dividers.

The special structure of a binder means that a person using the binder on their iPad can understand references to the lever-arch folder and vice versa. This allows some people to use the binder on their iPad while at the same time other people in the same court room use the binder printed out and in the lever-arch folder. For example, saying out loud "Your Honour will find that case behind tab 3" will allow a person using the binder on their iPad to instantly go to the same place as a person using the binder in a lever-arch folder.

The special structure of a binder makes it easy to print a bundle of authorities to be inserted into a lever-arch folder *and insert a cover sheet, table of contents and dividers*. Instructions on how to print a binder to be inserted into a lever-arch folder are explained in a separate guide (forthcoming - check back regularly).

The screenshots in this guide are from *Adobe Acrobat X Pro for Mac*, but this is very similar to version *XI Pro* and also very similar to versions X and XI for *Windows*. The concepts are also quite common in other PDF manipulation software.

I welcome feedback.

I recommend two types of useful tags: the first is a tag titled !To Be Curated. This performs the same function as the Inbox notebook for those of you who do not wish to have an Inbox notebook. The other type of tags I would recommend are years in numerals (e.g., 2013, 2014, 2015) and months in the form of both numerals and words (e.g., 01 January, 02 February, 03 March, etc.). Personally, I am very good at remembering where and when I had an idea. If I apply years and months tags to notes, it is a quick way of browsing to the relevant time that I recall making the note.

7.6 John Harding

John Harding is a family law trial lawyer and divorce mediator. He is the principal of Harding & Associates Family Law, with offices in Pleasanton and Walnut Creek, California. John is a Fellow in the American Academy of Matrimonial Lawyers and the International Academy of Matrimonial Lawyers. He is the publisher of the "California Divorce" blog (www.californiadivorceblawg.com) and the Family Law Lawyer Tech & Practice blog (www.familylawyertech.blogspot.com).

How John Uses Evernote in His Law Practice

Evernote is an essential information organizer. The genius of the program is its ability to transform all of my records into fully searchable records. Being able to pinpoint a specific document or record by simply typing in a keyword or two is brilliant.

As the owner of a small law firm, I find myself handling administrative tasks more than I would like. Evernote is an invaluable tool in this regard. I have created a personnel notebook in Evernote in which I store all resumes that I receive, all job applications, and all hiring papers. Each week, my employees e-mail their timesheets to me. I save those e-mails to Evernote with the convenient Microsoft Outlook add-on so that those timesheets also become part of each employee's personnel file in Evernote.

Evernote has eliminated my steel file cabinet filled with paper records that go along with running a law firm. Insurance policies, leases, equipment contracts, all get scanned and saved to Evernote.

E-mails from vendors, travel confirmations, just about everything is saved in Evernote. When I pay bills each week, those records are scanned and saved to Evernote. All of the paper archiving has been replaced with electronic archiving in Evernote.

That leads me to scanning. We utilize Fujitsu ScanSnap desktop scanners extensively in our practice. They are brilliant little machines. Most importantly for Evernote users, ScanSnap scanners have an Evernote link that is included in the resident software for the machines. With just a couple of mouse clicks, documents and records are scanned, stored, and indexed in Evernote. The seamless integration of Evernote and ScanSnap is an incredible model of efficiency.

As most lawyers will agree, we are constantly finding articles, stories, reports that we want to read later, or save for future reference. Be they paper or online, it was always a chore to save them, and to find them. A chore until Evernote came along. Now I just clip and save from the Internet to Evernote, or scan and save to Evernote. Evernote has developed a browser add-on that reduces this saving process to a couple of mouse clicks. Then the materials are saved as fully searchable PDF files. Another brilliant feature.

All of these functions are even more rewarding given Evernote's cross-platforming. I have Evernote installed on my PC at the office. I have the Evernote app installed on my iPhone. I have Evernote installed on the MacBook Pro that I carry with me everywhere. Everything that I could ever need or want from Evernote is available to me once, twice, three times! Anytime, anywhere.

Of course, running a successful law practice also requires other collateral activities such as bar associations, professional societies, networking groups, etc. Those activities generate their own e-mails and paper. Before Evernote, they were stored in Windows folders on an office computer. Searching and indexing was difficult. Access was an issue unless I was in the office. Now those items go straight to Evernote.

E-mail, e-mails, e-mails. E-mail is now the default means of communication. I e-mail my clients. My clients e-mail me. My vendors, friends, and colleagues e-mail me. E-mails related to cases were archived by our case management system. All the rest went into a saved items folder in Outlook. Then by the power of my memory and the time it took to surf through all of them, I could find messages when I needed them. Evernote has brought order to that e-mail chaos. With the Outlook add-on that Evernote has developed, a single click sends those collateral e-mails to my Evernote account. There they are indexed and searchable. Far more secure, far more organized, and far more useful.

The free version of Evernote is a great place to start. Once you begin to learn and use the program, it takes on a life of its own. The need to use it more and more takes over. It becomes an addiction by merit. It earns the right to become an obsession, and the need for more features and capacity increases. The Premium version with its unlimited storage and additional power user features is clearly the way to go, and well worth the nominal cost. My subscription is on auto pay, and I don't even question the cost. That is how important Evernote is to me.

John's Best Practice Tips

Business cards are still a great marketing tool. They are not virtual, they are tangible. You can touch them, feel them, and smell them. They work to market you and your practice, and they work to expand your networks. Handing them out is still an essential element of professional practice marketing. Collecting business cards is still an essential element in developing your business network.

Whether you use Microsoft's Outlook, Salesforce, Apple Contacts, AbacusLaw, Amicus Attorney, or Goldmine, etc., you need to get those business card buddies, and their business card information into your computerized contacts directory. In days gone by, that meant typing the information, line by line, into your computer. Now you can implement better technology to streamline the process of handling those business cards that you are collecting.

Evernote has some awesome business card tools. With the Evernote app on your smartphone you can take a picture of a business card, have it immediately imported into your Evernote account, export it to your contacts on your phone, and then synchronize it with your Outlook directory or any other contact management program that you use. Fear not, reading these steps is more complicated than doing the real thing. For some of these client management programs—Salesforce, for example—it is even easier because they have a dedicated Evernote interface. Even if you have to do it the multistep way without a dedicated interface, it is still incredibly easy. Keep reading to learn how.

Step One: Install Evernote on your smartphone.

Step Two: Lay a business card down on a flat surface.

Step Three: Launch Evernote on your smartphone, click on the Camera icon, and then select the Business Card option.

Step Four (see Figure 7.6): Move your camera over the business card until Evernote detects it and then automatically takes the picture for you.

FIGURE 7.6
Step Four

Step Five (see Figure 7.7): Evernote then reads the business card and imports all of the information as a new contact in your Evernote account. Nothing for you to do but watch.

Step Six: Tell Evernote to send the information to the Contacts app on your phone. Evernote completes the task immediately, and that business card buddy's information is now in your system.

Step Seven: Synchronize your phone contacts with whatever other Contact program(s) you use. Nothing could be easier.

Step Eight: Sit back and enjoy your techie awesomeness!

FIGURE 7.7
New Contact

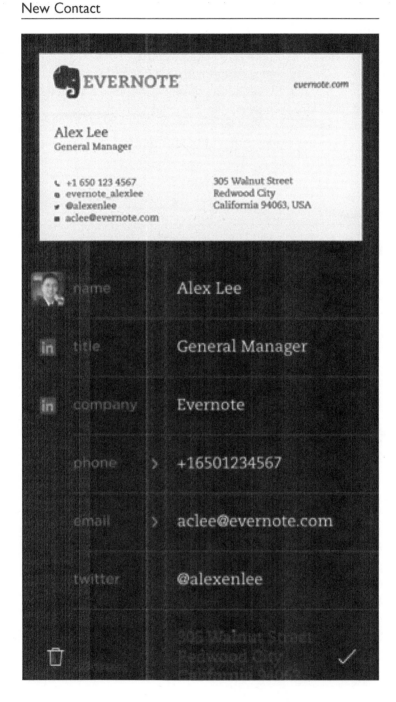

Bonus Tip: If you have a LinkedIn account, Evernote has a one-click feature so that you can connect on LinkedIn with your new business card buddy. After you have finished importing the business card and saving it in Evernote, Evernote will launch a pop-up window with a one-click LinkedIn button. If your new biz card buddy has a LinkedIn account, Evernote finds that account and then sends a LinkedIn connection request to that person. How great is that? This is an example of how software makers are getting away from the old proprietary, keep-'em-to-ourselves mentality, and instead they are embracing the benefits of platform sharing. The Evernote/Salesforce and Evernote/LinkedIn partnerships are examples. They expand their user base, and we the users expand the benefits of our accounts.

7.7 Jeffrey Lewis

Jeffrey Lewis is a partner at Broedlow Lewis LLP (www.broedlow lewis.com) in Southern California. He represents individuals and businesses in complex litigation, both at the trial and appellate levels. Jeff is also a certified appellate specialist by the California State Bar Board of Legal Specialization.

How Jeff Uses Evernote in His Law Practice

Evernote is an essential organizational tool for my business litigation and appellate practice. When a new matter comes into the office, a new Evernote notebook is immediately created for the matter. The notebook syncs with Rocket Matter, the firm's practice management software. The initial documents provided by the client (usually a contract, a real estate deed, or both) are scanned and added straight to Evernote. The initial interview of the client is accompanied by notes taken on the iPad with the Penultimate App, which syncs with Evernote. Later on, that interview is then available firm-wide on any computer, iPad, or iPhone running Rocket Matter. As the case progresses, Evernote is used to compile and organize notes and evidence about the case. A site visit to real property will result in photographs taken on the iPhone added straight to Evernote, along with annotations regarding key points in the photograph. If I only have time to scribble a quick note on a Post-It note, that note is eventually scanned and added to Evernote. All of the firm's legal research is compiled in separate Evernote notes with headings and tags to call the note up at a later date for any case. For example, a case establishing standing for a citizens group to challenge a zoning application is tagged with the terms "Research," "Standing," and "Land Use" for easy access later on for any of the firm's land use matters. A list of potential motion in limine topics is started at the beginning of the case and available firm-wide to all of the firm's lawyers to edit as the trial date progresses. Witness examination outlines for deposition and trial can be created and edited in Evernote. Images of the exhibits to be used during examination can be embedded inline into the note. When it comes to the actual examination at deposition or trial, the same note is accessed on an iPad. Questions can be ticked off as they are asked. Opening statements and closing arguments are also included in the Evernote notebook. The statements and arguments can be edited on the fly on the iPad or with a laptop back at the office.

Jeff's Best Practice Tip

On an Apple computer, if you right-click a PDF file, you have the option to Share to Evernote. This allows quick addition of key files to Evernote that can be tagged later.

7.8 Cat Moon

Cat Moon is a lawyer in Tennessee and blogger at the Inspired Law Blog (www.inspiredlawblog.com), where she helps other lawyers design what she calls an inspired law practice. She also runs Inspired Communicator (www.inspiredcommunicator.com), providing communications strategy, change management, and conflict resolution coaching and consulting services to educators.

How Cat Uses Evernote in Her Law Practice

Research

Evernote is a dream for research. I use many online sources for collecting statutory and transaction-related research, primarily. With the Evernote Web Clipper, any information I find is but a click away. I create notebooks for specific types of information (such as Tennessee Statutes) and then tag a note based on the content being saved, including by client name (see Figure 7.8). This lets me slice and dice the content—easy to find whatever I'm looking for, at a moment's notice.

FIGURE 7.8
Saving and Tagging Legal Research

Database for Important Information

All of the important information (that I don't need until I really need it) lives in Evernote, such as license codes for all the software I use and user guides and manuals for all the hardware I use (e.g., copier, scanner). (See Figure 7.9.) I also use Evernote to document various

FIGURE 7.9
Save Software Licenses

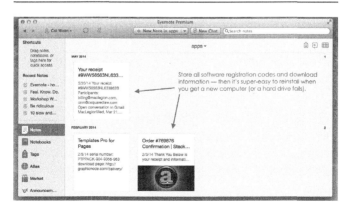

processes and procedures used in running my practice, such as how client intake is handled. These notes are shared with staff and can be updated by anyone involved in the process/procedure based on what is or isn't working in real time (which is one way my team implements kaizen, e.g., continual improvement).

Database for Forms and Templates

I've been creating and tweaking documents throughout my 17+ years of practice, to develop forms and templates I use on a daily basis. I store all of these in Evernote, tagging based on content. I also make notes on the various forms within Evernote, relevant to their application in actual practice. This enables me to quickly and efficiently create new documents for clients, drawing on past experience. Evernote's memory is much better than mine!

Cat's Best Practice Tips

Start Using It to Figure Out How It Best Serves Your Practice

I've lost count of the number of people who tell me that they've tried Evernote but just can't figure out how it works. When I push them to describe their experience with Evernote, it's typically clear that they used it for a day or two and then never experimented with it again. Like any other tool in your practice, you've got to use Evernote to figure out how it can serve you. Start saving your research into it. Start documenting your processes. Start saving your forms and templates into it. Try other things. My prediction? You'll find it to be an irreplaceable tool, very quickly.

Be Consistent in Using Evernote

The incredible value is the content it holds—you have to put stuff in it, to get stuff out of it. The more consistent you are in using Evernote to store the information you need most, the more you will benefit from it.

Encrypt Notes with Sensitive Content

I personally don't use Evernote to store client data. If you do want to store sensitive information (passwords, for example), you can encrypt individual notes for an added layer of security.

Use Evernote to Share Information Easily

Sharing a note or notebook is a fast, easy way to share *a lot* of content. Put a data-heavy PDF into Evernote, and share the note—instead of clogging up someone's e-mail inbox with a huge file. It's also a great way to share pictures (which are also storage hogs). It's an easy way to collaborate with a colleague or client on a project, as well—you can share draft documents, make notes, and communicate using Evernote's chat feature.

7.9 Jacob Small

Jacob Small is an employment lawyer based in McLean, Virginia, a technology and Mac enthusiast, and a novice computer programmer. He's written about the Fourth Amendment and cloud computing, and he has been interviewed by The Verge regarding cloud technology and the attorney-client privilege. Jacob is the founder and sole lawyer at J. Madison PLC (www.jmadisonplc.com).

How Jacob Uses Evernote in His Law Practice

I use Evernote for many purposes, but I primarily use it as an evidence database and trial notebook. When using Evernote this way, I create a single notebook for each case, and I place each piece of evidence (documents, pictures, audio files, e-mails, etc.) in a single note. First, I change each note's creation date to reflect the evidence contained therein. Then, I use tags and Evernote's advanced search syntax to organize evidence and find the evidence I need on the fly.

Here's how this works in practice. When I receive evidence from a client or in a document production, it's often in paper form or in a form that's easily converted to PDF. All paper is scanned to searchable PDF and put into my evidence processing workflow. Then, documents are split into discrete PDF documents—one PDF file per discrete piece of evidence—and Bates numbered as a batch using Adobe Acrobat. Acrobat also renames the files to match the range of Bates numbers stamped on the pages inside the PDF. Thus, a PDF file with a three-page document stamped with SMITH–000001 through SMITH–000003 will be named "SMITH–000001-SMITH–000003.pdf."

Moving these documents into Evernote is the next step, and it's easy. I simply drag the numbered and named PDF files into

Evernote, and Evernote creates the new notes, one note per PDF. The notes are automatically named by Evernote; each note has the same name as the file it contains, without the .pdf extension. This comes in handy later.

At this point, it's a good idea to attach some tags to the new notes to keep track of work that needs to be done to prepare the evidence for litigation. For example, I attach the tags needs dating, needs deduplication, needs issue tagging, needs witness tagging, and needs privilege check to every piece of evidence I import. I can do this in batches, as shown in Figure 7.10.

Then, for each process that I want to apply, I (1) search for all tags in a notebook that contain the tag, (2) perform the required process (i.e., identifying a date on the piece of evidence and modifying Evernote's Created attribute to reflect the date on the evidence), then (3) remove that processing tag from the note to reflect that the piece of evidence no longer needs to be processed in that way.

So what's the end result? After I've performed all processes on a batch of evidence, every piece of evidence in my database contains the following information: (1) an appropriate date, (2) a Bates number, (3) issue tags (these correspond with the elements of the claims and defenses in the lawsuit), and (4) witness tags. Also, Evernote allows me to mark duplicates and privileged documents and exclude them from search results. Therefore, when I've finished processing evidence, I can perform a powerful combination of searching and sorting.

FIGURE 7.10
Batch Tags for Processing

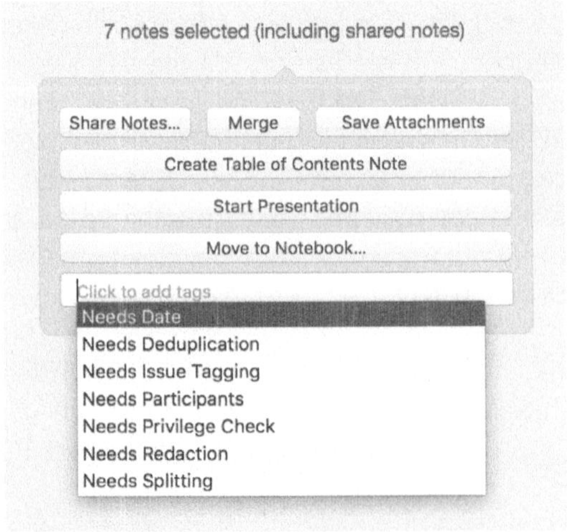

For example, I can see every piece of evidence—excluding duplicates and privileged documents—that addresses the damages element and that relates in some way to witness John Doe. If I'd like, I can then restrict that search to documents between two dates and sort it by either date or Bates number. From there, I can even dig deeper by looking within that batch for evidence that contains a specific search term in the body of the PDF.

For my employment litigation practice, this is very powerful.

Jacob's Best Practice Tips

1. I change the viewing mode in Evernote to Side List View. This makes it simple to scroll quickly through evidence that's sorted by Bates number or date, allowing me to easily navigate large batches of evidence. See Figure 7.11 for how to change your viewing mode.

FIGURE 7.11
Change Viewing Mode

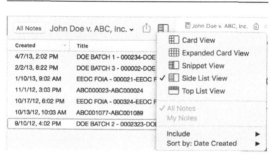

2. If you want to take full advantage of Evernote as an evidence database, you should take the time to read about Evernote's advanced search syntax, available here: https://help.evernote.com/hc/en-us/articles/208313828. For example, if I want to find every piece of evidence that is (1) related to witness Steven Smith; (2) created between July 22, 2013, and February 11, 2014; (3) contains the search string "haras"; and (4) excludes duplicates and privileged documents, I'd use this search string:

> created:20130722 -created:20140211 -tag:"Privileged"
> -tag:"Duplicate" tag:"Steven Smith" haras

Take this functionality a step further by creating shortcut snippets in the software program TextExpander for frequently used search strings, like -tag:"Privileged" -tag:"Duplicate."

3. Not only is Evernote great for understanding and organizing your evidence, but it is also helpful for responding to discovery. You can add tags to evidence to mark it as responsive to a particular request for production. For example, a document that is responsive to ABC, Inc.'s Request for Production Number 22 might have a tag called ABCRFP22.

Then, use Evernote to quickly generate responses. I do this with a four-step process. First, I do a search for every responsive document. That search would look like this: tag:"ABCRFP22." Second, I select all responsive documents and save the attachments to a folder that will later be produced to opposing counsel. Third, I create a Table of Contents note. The Table of Contents note contains a list of the responsive documents, and that list can simply be dropped into your draft discovery responses. Figures 7.12 and 7.13 show the Save Attachments and Table of Contents features.

FIGURE 7.12
Select Documents and Save Attachments

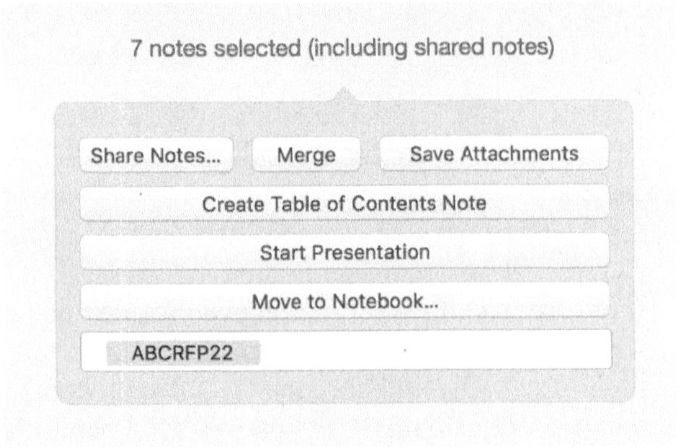

7 notes selected (including shared notes)

Share Notes...   Merge   Save Attachments

Create Table of Contents Note

Start Presentation

Move to Notebook...

ABCRFP22

FIGURE 7.13
Example Table of Contents

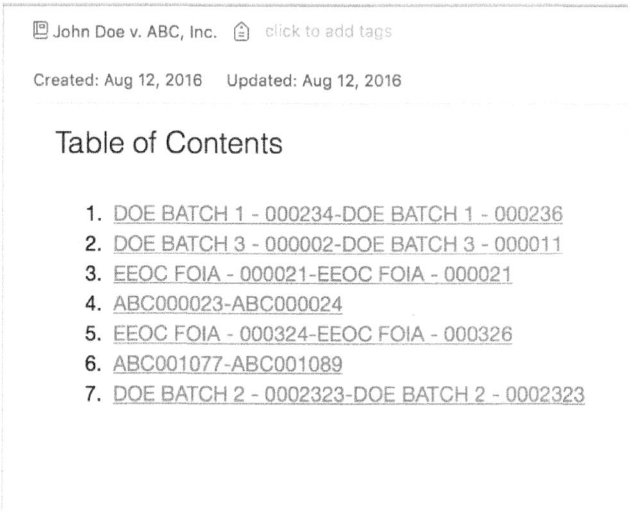

John Doe v. ABC, Inc. click to add tags

Created: Aug 12, 2016   Updated: Aug 12, 2016

Table of Contents

1. DOE BATCH 1 - 000234-DOE BATCH 1 - 000236
2. DOE BATCH 3 - 000002-DOE BATCH 3 - 000011
3. EEOC FOIA - 000021-EEOC FOIA - 000021
4. ABC000023-ABC000024
5. EEOC FOIA - 000324-EEOC FOIA - 000326
6. ABC001077-ABC001089
7. DOE BATCH 2 - 0002323-DOE BATCH 2 - 0002323

For me, the ability to sort through thousands of pieces of evidence to find just what I want is vital. In my search for a good software tool to manage evidence databases, I found high-priced software for Windows PCs, but nothing good for the Mac. Evernote fills that gap for me, and I'm very happy with the functionality it adds to my practice.

Appendix

Evernote Service Levels—Basic, Plus, Premium, and Evernote Business

As with many cloud-based services, Evernote offers a Basic (free) account for new and infrequent users, and more robust paid options for users looking to get more out of the service. Those options include Plus and Premium. Beyond that, there is a business solution, Evernote Business, which I'll discuss at the end of this section.

Once you have experimented with your Basic (free) Evernote account and begin to use the service more frequently, you may want to upgrade to a Plus or Premium account. While Evernote provides all users with unlimited total storage, each type of account has a separate monthly upload limit. In my opinion, this is the number one reason to upgrade your account. With a Basic account, your monthly upload limit is 60 MB. Your monthly upload limit includes any actions taken within your account that sync with Evernote's servers. This might include saving new content to your Evernote account, editing a note or an attachment, or adding/deleting images within a note. If you use Evernote frequently, you'll soon run up against the 60-MB limit. The Plus account bumps up your limit to 1 GB per month, while a Premium account gives you 10 GB per month.

There are many other differences between Basic, Plus, and Premium accounts. For a complete listing, see the Evernote pricing page: https://evernote.com/pricing/ and an Evernote Help & Learning article, available at https://help.evernote.com/hc/en-us/articles/209005157. Notable differences include the following:

- Note Size: Each type of account places a certain limit on the size of individual notes. Text within the note won't eat up your limit, but an image, PDF, or attachment may. Here are the limits: Basic—25 MB, Plus—50 MB, and Premium—200 MB.
- Notebook Limits: For Basic, Plus, and Premium accounts, the number of personally created notebooks is capped at 250. However, Plus and Premium account holders can join up to 500 shared notebooks, whereas Basic users can only join up to 100.
- Offline Notebooks: Only Plus and Premium accounts can be configured to access notes (from synced, not local notebooks) on mobile devices without an Internet connection. You have the option to select which notebooks to download for viewing offline. It's important to remember that downloading offline notebooks will use up space on your device.
- Sync: Basic users are limited to syncing data across two devices, whereas Plus and Premium account holders can sync to an unlimited number of devices.
- Annotation: PDF annotation is available only for Premium users. For more on annotation, see Section 2.6 of this book.
- Search Functionality: All account options allow users to search images, including handwritten and printed text. However, only Premium account users can search image-based/scanned PDFs and attachments. Learn more about search in Section 3.7.
- Context: Available only for Premium users, this feature searches your Evernote notebooks, your LinkedIn network, and other context sources, in real time (as you type), to provide you with information and resources relevant to the note you are currently viewing. Premium users can turn this feature on or off in the Preferences/Options pane and select context sources (including the *Wall Street Journal*, TechCrunch, Inc., *Forbes*, and more).

- E-Mails to and from Evernote: Only Plus and Premium accounts provide a dedicated Evernote e-mail address for saving e-mails directly into your Evernote account. You can send 200 e-mails per day to your Evernote account. For e-mails sent using Evernote's share feature, the allotment is 200 daily for Plus and Premium accounts, and 50 daily for Basic accounts. See Sections 3.3 and 3.6 for more information about sharing and saving via e-mail.
- Two-Step Verification: Two-step verification is available for all types of accounts, but only Plus and Premium support text message verification. See Section 6.3 for more information about two-step verification.
- Note History: Premium accounts allow you to restore previous versions of your notes. Evernote takes snapshots of your notes a few times a day. If you'd like to revert back to an older version, you can select the particular version and then click on Import to restore. When restoring, the previous version will not replace the current version; rather, it saves the previous version to a new Import notebook. Note History works on Mac and Windows desktop, as well as the web platform. You can view your note history by selecting the Information icon from the Note menu.
- Multiple Account Sign-In: Premium users can switch between multiple Evernote Premium accounts and one Basic or Plus account. On the desktop platform, click on your account name to sign into other accounts and then click on each account to switch between them.
- Support: All users can access the Evernote guides, Help & Learning site, and community forum. E-mail support is available for Plus and Premium users. Live chat support is available for Premium users only.

Evernote Business

For small to mid-size firms, Evernote Business can take a paperless office to the next level. With Evernote Business, you'll get all the features of a Premium account, as well as unique administrative and collaboration features. Individual users can view and join notebooks from a shared business library, share content and communicate with other colleagues, post content for the entire firm to view or collaborate, and create private notebooks for personal use. Evernote Business also provides dedicated business support services via e-mail, chat, or telephone, and additional security features, such as Single Sign-On (which works with third-party identity services to standardize security protocols for all users), administrative controls to manage user access, permanent data deletion, and more. You can learn more about Evernote Business security features at this web page: https://.evernote.com/security/business-features/. Evernote Business also integrates with Salesforce, a popular customer relationship management tool with solutions for law firms.

Integrations

There are hundreds (maybe thousands) of applications, most developed by third-party developers, that integrate with Evernote. You can discover many of these apps via Evernote's app center (https://appcenter.evernote.com). Apps that appear in Evernote's app center have been reviewed by Evernote.

Here are some apps and integrations you may find helpful:

- Alfred: Run this powerful Mac search tool with an Evernote workflow, and you can search, open, create notes, and more using a few keystrokes and without ever opening Evernote.
- CoSchedule: Plan, create, and publish content from Evernote with this web-marketing tool.
- DocuSign, EchoSign, and HelloSign: Access Evernote notes from these apps for electronic signature and then save signed notes back to Evernote. For Android, iOS, and web.
- Drafts: Save notes from Drafts (iOS app) directly to Evernote, append notes from Drafts to Evernote notes, create to-do lists in Evernote from Drafts, and more by creating your own actions from Drafts to Evernote.
- Expensify: Automatically add receipts, invoices, and other bills from Evernote to Expensify's expense management

program and send reports from Expensify to save in Evernote. For Android, iOS, and web.

- Feedly Pro and Reeder 2: Save articles from your Feedly or Reeder 2 web content aggregator directly to Evernote with one click. For Android, iOS, Mac, and web.
- FileThis: Automatically send online billing statements to Evernote. Statements are automatically tagged and organized into appropriate notebooks. For Android, iOS, and web.
- GotDone: Track your time with this web app that syncs with multiple services to log all your work, including from Evernote.
- Instapaper and Pocket: Save articles from read-later services, Instapaper and Pocket, directly to Evernote.
- Lightly: Use this app on your iPhone to strip hard-to-read web pages for better viewing, save simplified web pages to Evernote, and highlight text while reading to save to Evernote.
- LinkedIn: Connect your Evernote account to LinkedIn; then, when scanning a business card to Evernote, that individual's LinkedIn profile information and photo are automatically added to the note, and you'll have the option to connect on LinkedIn.
- Mail Butler: Enables easy conversion of Apple e-mail to Evernote notes with options for formatting, selecting notebooks, adding tags, and creating reminders.
- Meshin Recall: Connect this Android calendar app to your Evernote account to create notes associated with events and share notes directly from the app.
- Penultimate: Take handwritten notes that sync with Evernote with this iPad app developed by Evernote.
- PowerBot for Gmail, Google Calendar, and Yahoo Mail: Connects your Gmail, Google Calendar, or Yahoo Mail to Evernote for saving e-mails into Evernote and for sharing notes or notebooks by e-mail.
- Rocket Matter: Add your Evernote credentials to Rocket Matter to sync Evernote notebooks to your Rocket Matter

case matters. Access PDF and text files of your Evernote notes from your Rocket Matter case files.

- Salesforce: Create and link notes to your Salesforce records. View and edit those notes within your Salesforce dashboard.
- Scannable: Scan documents, receipts, and business cards with this mobile scanning app developed by Evernote for iPhone and iPad. This app automatically recognizes the type of document, adjusts the image, converts multiple pages into a single document, and saves it to Evernote (in PDF or JPEG format).
- Shoeboxed: Send paper documents, receipts, and business cards to this company, which will scan and sort your documents into your Evernote account.
- SnapCal: Connect this iPhone calendar app to send calendar events to Evernote and link existing calendar events with Evernote notes.
- Sunrise Calendar: Use the Sunrise Calendar app to sync reminders to Evernote (and vice versa; i.e., two-way sync). Add a Reminder to one app, and it will appear in the other. For Android, iOS, and web.
- UberConference: Share Evernote notes during an UberConference call. You can also save call logs to your Evernote account.
- Zapier and IFTTT: Use Zapier and IFTTT to connect Evernote to other applications and automate actions. For example, you can use these apps to turn Evernote note reminders to Google Calendar events. You could also use the services as an e-mail workaround for Basic users, connecting Evernote to Gmail to save e-mails from Gmail into Evernote.

Index

Alfred, 146
American Bar Association's
  Law Technology Resource
  Center, 100
Android platform, 4, 75, 76, 146–148
annotation
  case management using, 89
  overview of, 17–19
  service level allowances for, 144
  summary feature of, 18–19
  tools for, 18
  of web content, 42
Apple. *See* iOS platform; Mac
applications
  desktop (*see* Mac; Windows PC)
  Evernote as (*see* Evernote)
  of Evernote in law practices (*see*
    law practice applications)
  integrating with Evernote, 85,
    133, 146–148
  mobile (*see* mobile applications)
archiving
  Archive notebook for, 21, 97–98,
    126–128
  closed matters, 90
  exporting to XML for, 112
article, web content saved as, 41
attachments
  adding to notes, 34–40, 76
  searching, 62
  See also documents; images; PDF
    files; web content
attorney notes, 88
audio, adding to notes, 34
auto-filing feature, 47, 123–124
Automator application, 48
auto-title feature, 76

backing up data, 109–115
Bahgat, Joseph, 118–119
best practice tips, 119, 120–121,
  122–124, 126–128, 130–133,
  134, 136–137, 139–141. *See*
  also Power User Tips
Blackberry platform, 4, 75
blog
  checklists for, 92, 94
  drafts of, 118–119
  Evernote, 5, 7
  marketing, 92
bookmarks, web content saved via, 42
Brother scanner, 47
browser. *See* web browser
business cards
  marketing use of, 93, 130
  scanning, 76–77, 130–133

calendar reminders. *See* reminders
Canon scanner, 47
Carter, Ben, 119–121
case examples. *See* real-life
    examples
case law
  case headnotes for, 125–126
  tagging, 119
case management, 85–90
  closed matters in, 90
  open matters in, 88–89, 133–134,
    137–139
  pending matters stack in,
    87–88
  security considerations in,
    85–86
  system design for, 86
case timeline, 88